Raising African-American Males

Strageties and Interventions for Successful Outcomes

Theresa L. Harris and George Taylor

ROWMAN & LITTLEFIELD EDUCATION
A division of
ROWMAN & LITTLEFIELD PUBLISHERS, INC.
Lanham • New York • Toronto • Plymouth, UK

Published by Rowman & Littlefield Education
A division of Rowman & Littlefield Publishers, Inc.
A wholly owned subsidary of The Rowman & Littlefield Publishing Group, Inc.
4501 Forbes Boulevard, Suite 200, Lanham, Maryland 20706
http://www.rowmaneducation.com

Estover Road, Plymouth PL6 7PY, United Kingdom

British Library Cataloguing in Publication Information Available

Library of Congress Cataloging-in-Publication Data

Harris, Theresa, 1956-
Raising African-American males : strategies and interventions for successful outcomes / Theresa
Harris and George Taylor.
p. cm.
Summary: "Raising African-American Males is comprised of strategies and interventions that can
assist and improve African American males' achievement in all areas of academics as well as in their
everyday lives. Theresa Harris and George Taylor provide pedagogical strategies that employ various
instructional tools for teachers, parents, African American youth, and administrators"—Provided by
publisher.
ISBN 978-1-60709-298-8 (hardback)—ISBN 978-1-60709-299-5 (paper)—ISBN 978-1-60709-300-
8 (electronic)
1. African American young men—Education. 2. African American men—Education. 3. Academic
achievement—United States. 4. Education—Parent participation—United States. 5. African
American young men—Family relationships. 6. African American young men—Social conditions. 7.
African American men—Social conditions. I. Taylor, George, 1944- II. Title.
LC2731.H37 2011
371.821'1--dc23
2011036902

♻™ The paper used in this publication meets the minimum requirements of American
National Standard for Information Sciences Permanence of Paper for Printed Library
Materials, ANSI/NISO Z39.48-1992.

Printed in the United States of America

This book is dedicated to one of the truest scholars whose legacy continues to advance the cause for African-American males. This scholar, Dr. Colonel Hawkins, has advanced the cause of the African-American males in a humanitarian way.

This book is also dedicated to Jomo Sundiata-Terry Miguel, Jamaun, Jayden, and Justin; to Matthew III, Andre Sr. and Jr., J. J., Little Frank, James, Jonathan, and Michael; and to all who are committed to the cause of supporting the positive outcomes for African-American males.

Contents

Preface

A variety of developments has occurred in urban education since its inception. Many of these developments have been a result of direct interventions designed to bring about education reform on behalf of educating African-American males in an urban setting. This book addresses the need for effective parental involvement, more extensive research on all fronts, and expansive community and professional organizational involvement to improve the quality of education for African-American males. Also, this book has been written to provide some of the more recent and promising trends. The book is particularly useful for school personnel and officials, parents, school psychologists, community agencies, the empowerment of African-American youth themselves, and researchers in the social sciences and other related fields. This represents a unified collaborative effort to improve the educational, social, economic, and moralistic opportunities for the successful integration of African-American males in society.

The book comprises ten chapters. Chapter 1 provides an introduction to the book. Chapter 2 presents standards-based life skills interventions and strategies. Chapter 3 summarizes societal and environmental factors affecting African-American males. Chapter 4 deals with drug education and awareness intervention strategies. In chapter 5, modeling themes for parental support are overviewed. Learning theories for parents are discussed in chapter 6. The employment of assessment strategies, as it relates to instruction and assessment outcomes, is covered in chapter 7. Chapter 8 represents a proposed model for closing the achievement gap for African-American males. Chapter 9 discusses the coordination and utilization of the community resources and related services. Chapter 10 is a summary of the collaborative works discussed throughout the book.

Chapter One

Introduction

In today's American society, there are a multiplicity of problems influencing the behavior and attitudes of young people. These influences have always been in society on some level, but the depth and complexity of modern-day influences, particularly negative influences, is of great importance. There are various forces in society that result in the accelerated numbers of African-American males' dilemmas in school, as well as the high rate of incarceration they face.

Many African-American males fear for their safety in their schools, their community, and society in general. Many fear the police and view them as dishonest. Based on many of their experiences, they have no belief in the American court system. Unless help for these youth, placed at risk for numerous reasons, is provided by their parents in collaboration with society, particularly positive community support, these youth will continue to be less than a viable, productive force in society. In simple terms, if something profound is not done to deter African-American males' perpetuation with social problems, society as a whole will suffer. Total collaborative efforts must come from the community and the state, and various forms of federal interventions must be developed and coordinated.

Problems for African-American males include substandard education, lack of efficacy in teaching them, community crisis as a whole, the need for coordinated efforts of mentorship, and the need to provide quality education to educate the "whole child." A report by the National Association of State Boards of Education[1] noted that a holistic view that is attuned to the student's nonacademic needs must be included as part of the student's instructional program. This includes social, emotional, and personal citizenship training.

Other researchers have voiced similar concerns[2] in support of a holistic integrated approach to educating children. It was recommended that to avoid fragmenting school experiences, students' social and emotional well-being must be integrated and infused into a total program emphasizing social and interpersonal needs, communication needs, and academic needs. The schools must begin to use the vast amount of research presented to experiment with various ways of including social skills development into the curriculum if African-American males are to achieve their maximum potential.

The concept of teaching the whole child has been advocated since the beginning of the century. Historically, the school has mainly focused on academics, not the emotional development of children. However, a body of research draws attention to the importance of emotions in teaching children. Attention, learning, and memory are all associated with one's emotions. This concept does not appear to be readily understood by educators; thus, it is not adequately reflected in the curriculum. School districts should conduct more empirical studies showing the relationship between an emotionally positive classroom and the academic achievement and emotional health of pupils.[3]

Cummings's[4] findings support educating the whole child. He advocates that current assessment models used to instruct African-American males are not based upon the learning and culture styles of these boys; thus, they frequently cannot achieve success. Radical intervention models are needed; parents cannot accomplish this awesome task alone. Parents in addressing educational problems must concurrently address deep-seated social problems. Children learn violent behaviors early. This is especially true for African-American males due chiefly to social, physical, and mental problems deeply rooted in their environments. Interventions need to start early, with three-year-olds or younger, to instruct and teach them more appropriate ways to handle frustration and anger.

Intervention strategies should be based upon skills needed for the youth that help them function successfully in society and better understand their self-worth. Additionally, African-American males must be provided with the necessary strategies and mental tools to keep them crime free. The parents' roles are essential in helping to decrease these problems. They must be given the training and support needed to effectively counsel their children and loved ones, as well as to demonstrate positive role modeling. When necessary, the parents should seek role models outside of the family who can provide positive exampling.

Youth must first know and understand the playing field. African-American youth must be given an understanding of the norms and values that impact them most. This is not to advocate that they become robotic, but that they fully understand the game from home, to their entry into school, to their entrance to jobs. Parental involvement is crucial in helping their children understand the playing field and thus reducing their incarceration rates.

Parents display a variety of reactions when they discover that their children are using drugs. As outlined by George Taylor,[5] parents should seek effective counseling techniques by competent counselors. They should be provided with (1) detailed information relevant to drug usage; (2) types of recommended treatment and diagnosis; (3) community facilities that treat addictions, including programs at school; (4) ways of modeling appropriate behavior for children to emulate; (5) suggestions for monitoring the boys' activities; (6) ways to question strange behaviors of the boys; (7) strategies for participating in family social activities and discussions concerning the harmful effects of drugs; (8) ways to employ a variety of interventions; (9) the location of community resources; (10) surveying community and state organizations; and (11) ways of making contacts with local, state, and federal funding agencies.

Positive parental involvement, coupled with positive involvement by school officials, parents, teachers, significant mentors, the community at large, churches, and other civic groups, supports the goal for the development of youth who sustain "positive and productive" lifestyles. The following five primary and essential ingredients support the positive societal advancement of African-American males:

1. Attaining successful goals taught as life skills in which youth learn to recognize their own intermittent and continuous successes, no matter how big or small. Parents, school officials, teachers, significant mentors, the community at large, churches, and other civic groups must acknowledge these successes. These positive behaviors must be reinforced as prominent and significant factors that receive some form of celebration. By celebrating and being rewarded for these intermittent successes, youths will learn to understand and embrace their own successes with positive rather than apocalyptic outlooks about their future.

2. Devaluing criminal attitudes, behaviors, and ideologies, particularly family patterns of attitudes and behaviors that have been transgenerational, that lead to and result in further incarcerations.

3. Understanding the playing field, including assumptions and nonassumptions. It is essential that youth are taught about inequalities and injustices.

4. Using self-correctedness and self-assessment strategies to keep youth focused in the right direction. Of course, positive guidance from positive role models is essential in this self-correctedness and self-assessment process.

5. Building life skills that are standards based, driven by positive role modeling from significant role models, is essential to the propensity that youth will remain positively focused. Positive role models are

considered positive because of the high standards they demonstrate. In the process of emulation, youth must be taught about the characteristics and standards that produce positive lifestyles and positive outcomes. Positive role modeling is essential because of the positive demonstration that can be seen and modeled by youth.

If a child's early development and early home environment are both affected by social factors resulting in low expectation and negative stigmatization, there is an increased likelihood of poor developmental outcomes. The home environment is the foundation to further positive development within the child. Thus, the home environment should be where the child receives support, experiences love, and acquires important skills toward becoming a productive, happy, social, and emotional person. Experiences from the home need to be integrated with the school curriculum for meaningful experiences to occur. This will necessitate including family and the community in the education process.[6] Parents must be trained to teach the youth appropriate social skills.

These are skills needed to help them live a law-abiding life and to bring them some measure of success and personal fulfillment. Hilliard[7] summed up the blight of urban education in this country by stating, "Nothing in school reform reports and effective research in general offers promise for the massive changes in education necessary to save the huge number of children in our systems that are at-risk." He concludes that the most at-risk segment of the school population is the black male.

NOTES

1. National Association of State Boards of Education, *Winners All: A Call for Inclusive Schools* (Alexandria, VA: National Association of State Boards of Education, 1992).

2. R. Bilken, "Making Differences Ordinary," in *Educating All Children in the Mainstream of Regular Education*, W. Stainback and M. Forest, eds. (Baltimore, MD: Paul H. Brooks, 1990); M. Forest, "Maps and Cities" (presentation at Peak Park Center Workshop, Colorado Springs, CO, 1990); R. Barth, *Improving Schools from Within* (San Francisco: Jossey-Bass, 1990); E. Eisner, *The Enlightened Eye* (New York: Macmillan, 1991); J. O'Brien and C. L. O'Brien, "Members of Each Other: Perspectives on Social Supports for People with Disabilities," in *Personal Relationships and Social Networks: Facilitating the Participation of Individuals with Disabilities in Community Life*, Z. M. Lutfiyya, ed. (Lithonia, GA: Responsive Systems Associates, 1991).

3. M. Kandel and E. Kandel, "Flights of Memory," *Discover Magazine* (1994): 32–38; J. P. Vincent, *The Biology of Emotions* (Cambridge: Blackwell, 1990).

4. J. Cummings, *Bilingual and Special Education: Issues in Assessment Pedagogy* (San Diego: College Hill Press, 1984).

5. G. R. Taylor, "Reforms in Educating African-American Males in Baltimore City Public Schools," in *The State of Black Baltimore*, J. H. Henderson and S. F. Battle, eds. (Baltimore: Coppin State University and the Greater Baltimore Urban League, 2004).

6. S. L. Kagan, "Early Care and Education: Beyond the Schoolhouse Doors," *Phi Delta Kappa* (1989): 107–12.

7. A. G. Hilliard, "Teachers and Culture Styles in a Pluralistic Society," *NEA Today* 6 (1989): 65–69.

Chapter Two

Standards-Based Life Skills Interventions

Direct intervention implies that the parent, teacher, and significant mentor are directing intervention to bring about a desired change. This strategy can be used with any task, concept, or subject area to assist African-American males in learning basic skills. McGinnis and Goldstein[1] support the concept of direct instruction of social skills by recommending the following strategies: modeling, role playing (practice and transfer of training), and skill-streaming. Other techniques include cognitive behavior modification, behavior modification techniques (coaching, social cognitive approaches), and cooperative learning and group activities.

MODELING

Modeling assumes that African-American males will imitate the behaviors displayed by others. The progress is considered important because youths acquire social skills through replicating behaviors demonstrated by others. Educators and adults may employ modeling techniques to change and influence inappropriate behaviors by demonstrating appropriate skills to model. Parents, teachers, and significant mentors, who frequently fail to assess the impact of their behaviors on children, often overlook the impact and importance of this valuable technique.[2]

Modeling, if used appropriately, may influence or change behaviors more effectively than the demonstration of behaviors. Consequently, many African-American males model behaviors they observe in their communities. This is premised upon the fact that once a behavior pattern is learned through imitation, it is maintained without employing positive reinforcement techniques. Parents, teachers, and significant mentors should be apprised and cognizant of the importance of modeling for promoting appropriate social skills. Additionally, they should be trained and exposed to various techniques to facilitate the progress.

African-American males do not automatically imitate the models they see. Several factors are involved: (1) establishing rapport between mentors and boys, (2) reinforcing consequences, and (3) determining the appropriate setting for modeling certain behaviors.[3]

African-American males should be taught how to show or demonstrate positive behaviors by observing others performing positive behaviors in structured situations. The techniques provide for the structured learning of appropriate behaviors through examples and demonstration by others. Internal or incidental modeling may occur at any time, and modeling activities may be infused throughout the curriculum at random. However, a regular structured time or period of day is recommended in order to develop structure in a variety of social conditions. Teaching behavioral skills through modeling is best accomplished by beginning with impersonal situations similar to those that most students encounter, such as the correct way to show respect for others. Activities should be planned based upon the assessed needs of the class and be flexible enough to allow for changes when situations dictate. As African-American males master the modeling process, additional behavioral problems may be emphasized.[4]

Videotape Modeling

Videotape modeling is an effective way to improve self-concept. African-American males may be encouraged to analyze classroom behavior and behavioral patterns of interaction through reviewing videotapes. In this way, children can see the expected behaviors before they are exposed to them in various settings. Videotape modeling affords parent, teacher, and significant mentors the opportunity to reproduce the natural conditions of any behavior in the classroom setting. Consequently, videotape modeling may provide realistic training that can be transferred to real experiences inside and outside of the classroom. For African-American males, educators may employ this technique to help transfer modeling skills to real-life situations. It has been proven as an effective tool to teach prosocial skills to this group.[5]

Black Role Models

Some authorities, in an effort to improve the education of African-American males, advocate an increase in the presence of African-American role models. It is believed that the presence of African-American role models can have a positive effect on the behavior of the boys.[6] Wright[7] also supports the above view by stating, "African-American males need legitimate African-American role models to develop their self-esteem." LaPoint concluded that African-American male adults must become new role models of empowerment and advocacy to African-American males to provide a fatherly image and to prevent them from succumbing to vices and the influences of illegal activities in their environments. [8]

African-American males need to see African-American role models with whom they can identify and whom they can emulate by seeing their role models' employment in worthy professions. They need to see these role models as intelligent, capable, worthy, and contributing citizens.

ROLE PLAYING

Role playing is an excellent technique for allowing African-American males to act out both appropriate and inappropriate behaviors without embarrassment or without experiencing the consequences of their actions. It permits students to experience hypothetical conditions that may cause anxiety or emotional responses in ways that may enable them to better understand themselves. Once entrenched, these activities may be transferred to real-life experiences.

Role playing may assist the boys in learning appropriate social skills through developing appropriate models by observing and discussing alternative behavioral approaches. Role playing may be conducted in any type of classroom structure, level, or group size. It may be individually or group induced. Through appropriate observations and assessment procedures, areas of intervention may be identified for role-playing activities.

Role playing assists African-American males in identifying and solving problems within a group context. It is also beneficial to shy students. It encourages their interactions with classmates without adverse consequences. As with most group activities, role playing must be structured. Activities should be designed to reduce, minimize, correct, or eliminate identified areas of deficits through the assessment process.

Gill listed the following advantages of role playing:

1. allows the boy to express hidden feelings;
2. addresses the needs and concerns of the student by being student centered;
3. permits the boys to control the content and pace;
4. enables the student to empathize with others and understand their problems;

5. portrays generalized social problems and dynamics of group interaction, formal and informal;
6. gives more reality and immediacy to academic descriptive material (history, geography, social skills, English);
7. enables the boys to discuss private issues and problems, provides an opportunity for inarticulate students, and emphasizes the importance of nonverbal and emotional responses;
8. gives practice in various types of behaviors.[9]

Disadvantages include:

1. The parent, teacher, or significant mentor can lose control over what is learned and the order in which it is learned.
2. Simplifications can mislead.
3. It may dominate the learning experiences to the exclusion of solid theory and facts.
4. It is dependent upon the personality, quality, and mix of the parent, teacher, significant mentor, and students.
5. It may be seen as too entertaining and frivolous.

Gill investigated the effects of role play, modeling, and videotape on the self-concept of elementary school children, 13 percent of whom were African-Americans. The Piers-Harris Children's Self-Concept Scale was employed on a pre- and posttest basis. Intervention was for a six-month period. Data showed that the combination of role playing, modeling, and videotape playback had some effect upon various dimensions of self-concept.[10] 0

SKILLSTREAMING

Skillstreaming is a comprehensive social skills program. Social skills are clustered in several categories with specific skills to be demonstrated to foster human interactions skills needed to perform appropriate social acts. Clear directions are provided for forming the skillstreaming groups, conducting group meetings, and specifying rules. Activities include modeling, role playing, feedback, and transfer training. Feedback received in the form of praise, encouragement, and constructive criticism is designed to reinforce correct performance of the skills.

COGNITIVE BEHAVIOR MODIFICATION

These techniques focus on having African-American males think about and internalize their feelings and behaviors before reacting. The process involves learning responses from the environment by listening to, observing, and imitating others. Both cognition and language processes are mediated in solving problems and developing patterns of behaviors.

Cognitive behavioral strategies are designed to increase self-control of behavior through self-monitoring, self-evaluation, and self-reinforcement. The strategies assist African-American males with internalizing their behaviors, comparing their behaviors against predetermined standards, and providing positive and negative feedback to themselves. Research findings indicate that there is a positive relationship between what individuals think about themselves and the types of behaviors they display. This premise appears to be true for African-American males as well. Matching the cognitive and affective processes in designing learning experiences for the individuals appears to be realistic and achievable within the school.

OPERANT AND BEHAVIOR MODIFICATION TECHNIQUES

Behavioral modification techniques provide the parent, teacher, significant mentor, or counselor with strategies for assisting African-American males in performing desirable and appropriate behaviors as well as promoting socially acceptable behaviors. It is a method to modify behavior to the extent that when a behavior is emitted in a variety of situations, it becomes consistently more appropriate.

Some cautions have been mentioned for parent, teacher, significant mentors, and counselors using behavioral strategies. The chief purpose of using this technique is to change or modify behaviors. The parent, teacher, significant mentor, or counselor is not generally concerned with the cause of the behaviors but rather with observing and recording overt behaviors. These behavioral responses can be measured and quantified in any attempt to explain behaviors. There are occasions, however, when motivation and the dynamic causes of the behaviors are primary concerns for the parent, teacher, significant mentor, or counselor.

In spite of the cautions involving the use of behavioral modification techniques, most of the research supports their use. The major concerns voiced were that the technique must be systematically employed; the environmental constraints must be considered; and parent, teacher, significant mentors, educators, counselors, and parents must be well versed in using the technique. This is especially true when used with African-American males.

Behavior can be modified in many ways. Contingency contracting, peer mediation, task-centered approaches, coaching, cueing, social-cognitive approaches, modeling, role playing, cooperative learning, special group activities, skillstreaming, and cognitive behavior modification are but a few techniques to employ in reducing inappropriate behavior of African-American males.

CONTINGENCY CONTRACTION

This technique involves pupils in planning and executing contracts. Gradually, pupils take over record keeping, analyze their own behavior, and even suggest the timing for cessation of contracts. Microcontracts are made with the pupil in which he agrees to execute some amount of low-probability behavior (Premack's principle) for a specified time. An example would be that an African-American male who likes to play sports will be denied the opportunity to play until homework assignments have been completed.

PEER MEDIATION STRATEGIES

Peer mediation strategies have been successfully employed to manage drug behaviors of children and youth. The model is student driven and enables African-American males to make decisions about issues and conflicts that have an impact upon their lives. The model requires that students exercise self-regulation strategies, which involve generating socially appropriate behavior in the absence of external control imposed by parent, teacher, significant mentors, or other authorities. To be effective, the concept must be practiced and frequently reinforced through role models and demonstrations or prosocial skills. A significant amount of inappropriate behavior may be attributed to peer pressure. This strategy promotes modeling appropriate behavior and denounces negative behaviors.

Several investigations have shown that negative behaviors and discipline problems decrease when this strategy is used. For example, an increase in cooperative relationships and academic advisement often follows. Findings also show an increase in task behaviors. By using this strategy, particularly with African-American males, appropriate behaviors are internalized and can assist them in refusing to engage in inappropriate behavior.

TASK-CENTERED APPROACH

The task-centered approach to learning is another way to modify negative behavior. Pupils may be experiencing difficulty because they cannot grasp certain social skills concepts. Behavioral problems may stem from the frustration of repeated failure, such as poor attention or the inability to work independently or in groups. This system provides African-American males a highly structured learning environment. Elements in the task-centered approach may include activities to promote:

1. attention-level tasks designed to gain and hold the pupil's attention;
2. development of visual and auditory discrimination activities as needed;
3. interpretation and reaction to social-level tasks emphasizing skills related to social interaction;
4. imitation of social exchanges, the development of verbal and social courtesies, and group participation activities.

COACHING

Appropriate coaching techniques may be employed by parent, teacher, significant mentors, and counselors to develop social skills for African-American males. Some of the commonly known techniques include: (1) participation, (2) paying attention, (3) cooperation, (4) taking turns, (5) sharing, (6) communication, and (7) offering assistance and encouragement. These techniques are designed to make individuals cognizant of using alternative methods of solving behavior problems, anticipating the consequences of their behaviors, and developing plans for successfully coping with problems.

CUEING

Cueing is employed to remind African-American males to act appropriately just before the correct action is expected rather than after an action is performed incorrectly. This technique is an excellent way of reminding them about prior standards and instruction. A major advantage is that it can be employed anywhere, using a variety of techniques such as glances, hand signals, pointing, nodding, shaking the head, or holding up the hand, to name but a few. Cueing can be utilized without interrupting the instructional program or planned activities. The technique assists in reducing negative practices and prevents the boys from performing inappropriate behaviors.

Successful implementation of this technique requires that the boys thoroughly understand the requirement as well as recognize the specific cue. Otherwise, the result might be confusing, especially when the boys are held accountable for not responding appropriately to the intended cue.

SOCIAL-COGNITIVE APPROACHES

These techniques are designed to instruct African-American males, help them maintain better control over their behaviors, and deal more effectively with social and drug matters through self-correction and problem solving. Self-mentoring or instruction involves verbal prompting by the boys concerning their social behavior. Verbal prompting may be overt and covert.

MAKING BETTER CHOICES

This social-cognitive approach is designed to assist African-American males in making better choices when considering acting inappropriately. Group lessons are developed around improving social skills. Specifically, lessons promote forethought before engaging in a behavior and development of the ability to examine the consequences of the behavior. The major components of this program include the following cognitive sequence:

1. Stop (inhibit response).
2. Plan (behaviors leading to positive behaviors).
3. Do (follow plan and monitor behavior).
4. Check (evaluate the success of the plan).

These steps are practiced by the boys and reinforced by the parent, teacher, significant mentor, and counselor. The parent, teacher, and significant mentor identify various social skills for the boys to practice. Progress reports are kept and assessed periodically by parent, teacher, significant mentors, and the boys.

COOPERATIVE LEARNING

A basic definition of cooperative learning is "learning through the use of groups." Five basic elements of cooperative learning are

1. positive interdependence;
2. individual accountability;
3. group processing;
4. small group/social skills;
5. face-to-face interaction.

A cooperative drug group is one in which two or more students work together toward a common goal in which every member of the group is included. Learning together in small groups has been shown to provide a sense of responsibility and an understanding of the importance of cooperation among African-American males. Children need to socialize and interact with each other. Among the best-known cooperative structures are jigsaw classrooms, Student Teams Achievement Divisions (STAD), think-pair-share techniques, group investigation, circle of learning, and simple structures.

Cooperative learning strategies have the power to show the boys how to deal successfully with negative behaviors. Decisions about the content of the structure and the current social skill development of the learners must be carefully considered. For successful outcomes with students, the parent, teacher, and significant mentors also need follow-up, peer coaches, administrative support, parent understanding, and time to adapt to the strategies.

Cooperative learning practices vary tremendously. The models can vary from complex to simple. Whatever their design, cooperative strategies include

1. a common goal;
2. a structured task;
3. a structured team;
4. clear roles;
5. a designated time frame;
6. individual accountability;
7. a structured process.

We need cooperative structures in our classrooms because many traditional socialization practices are absent. Not all students come to school with a social orientation, and students appear to master content more efficiently with these structures. The preponderance of research indicates that cooperative learning strategies motivate students to care about each other and to share responsibility in completing tasks; this is especially true for African-Americans.

SPECIAL GROUP ACTIVITIES

In a paper presented at the annual meeting of the American Education Research Association, Dorr-Bremme advanced some unique techniques for improving social identity in kindergarten and first grade. Students sat in groups and planned daily activities; these activities were videotaped. Analysis of the videotapes revealed several dimensions of social identity that are important, such as academic capability, maturity, talkativeness, independence, aggressiveness, ability to follow through, and leadership ability. The parent, teacher, and significant mentor responded to students individually and as circle participants, depending upon how the behavior was viewed.

Findings indicated that social identity was the combined responsibility of everyone in the classroom interacting to bring about the most positive social behavior. Interactions between individual students and the parent, teacher, and significant mentor were minimized. The implications for using special group activities with African-American males are clear from the above research findings.

THE ROLE OF THE SCHOOL IN A BEHAVIORAL SETTING

A meaningful approach to dealing with inappropriate behaviors would be to isolate the behavior and then qualify, record, and observe the number of acts involved. When this determination has been made, the parent, teacher, significant mentor, or counselor is equipped to undertake a course of action to change the negative behavior. Social skills training is the technique advocated.

African-American males enter school with a wide range of interests, motivation, personality, attitudes, cultural orientations, and socioeconomic status. These traits and abilities must be recognized and incorporated into the instructional program. The boys also enter school with set behavioral styles. Frequently, these styles are inappropriate for the school. Several techniques are recommended to change inappropriate behaviors in the classroom:

1. Raise the tolerance of the parent, teacher, and significant mentor. Parents, teachers, and significant mentors generally expect pupils to perform up to acceptable standards. Additionally, they often assume that

pupils have been taught appropriate social skills at home. Whereas this may be true for most pupils, frequently it is not true for African-American males. By recognizing causal factors, such as environment, culture, and values, the parent, teacher, and significant mentor's tolerance level may be raised.

2. Change parent, teacher, and a significant mentor's expectations for pupils. Pupils generally live up to parents', teachers', and significant mentors' expectations. Parents, teachers, and significant mentors should expect positive behaviors from children. To accomplish this goal, behaviors will sometimes have to be modeled. It is also recommended that individual time be allowed for certain pupils through interviews and individual conferences where the parent, teacher, and significant mentor honestly relate how the child's behavior is objectionable.

3. Analyze parent, teacher, and significant mentor's behavior toward a pupil. Pupils use parent, teacher, and significant mentor's overt behavior as a mirror of their strength in the classroom. When a positive reflection is projected, the achievement level is increased. When the message is overtly negative, the pupil has nothing to support his efforts. For example, if there is little positive interaction between the pupil and the parent, teacher, and significant mentor, the pupil may conclude that the parent, teacher, and significant mentor do not approve of his behavior. Because the pupil depends so heavily on the parent, teacher, and significant mentor's behavior for clues, it is crucial that the parent, teacher, and significant mentor objectively analyze his or her interaction with the pupils.

SUMMARY

Research findings have shown that African-American males of lower socioeconomic status are significantly more likely to demonstrate inappropriate behaviors than other groups of students because of the living styles and stresses imposed by their living environments. The available pool of minority parents, teachers, and significant mentors is declining. This is unfortunate because the literature has shown that African-American males are in desperate need of male role models. Without these role models, boys from high-risk environments may emulate inappropriate models to which they have been exposed. A significant amount of inappropriate behavior is learned operant behavior; when positive models are introduced, negative behaviors are significantly reduced.

More minority parents, teachers, and significant mentors are needed to meet the needs of increasing numbers of African-American and other minority groups. More than one-third of America's schoolchildren are members of a minority group, while the majority of parents, teachers, and significant mentors are white. Approximately 16 percent of the nation's public school population is African-American, but only 7 percent of the public school teaching force is African-American.[11]

A variety of intervention strategies may be used to improve performance of African-American males, depending upon their assessed and diverse needs. Interventional strategies should be adapted to take into account these diverse needs. It is hoped that proposed legislation by the Obama administration recommending that same-sex classes be approved, will enable school districts to provide separate classes for instructing African-American males.

The goals of education for all children are to assist them in becoming competent and well-adjusted individuals, now as well as in the future, by creating an atmosphere that supports learning. For such education to be effective, children must share this philosophy, and they must have an essential part in developing it through communicating their interests.

NOTES

1. G. R. Taylor, *Curriculum Strategies: Social Skills Intervention for Young African-American Males* (Westport, CT: Greenwood, 1997): 10, 21; J. Brown, "Coleman School's All-Male Class a Success," *Baltimore Sun*, June 12, 1991, D1–3; C. R. Gibbs, "Project 2000: Why Black Men Should Teach Black Boys," *Dollars & Sense*, February/March 1991, 18–28; P. G. Graham, "Black Teachers: A Drastically Scarce Resource," *Phi Delta Kappa* 68 (1987): 595–605.

2. D. Ruenzel, "War of Attrition," *Education Week* 18 (September, 1998): 33–35.

3. A. Bandura and R. Walters, *Social Learning and Personality Development* (New York: Holt, Rinehart and Winston, 1963).

4. Taylor (1997):45–46.

5. G. R. Taylor, *Practical Application of Social Learning Theories in Educating Young African-American Males* (Lanham, MD: University Press of America, 2003): 45.

6. J. W. Gibbs, *Young, Black, and Male in America: An Endangered Species* (Dover: Auburn Publishing, 1998); Gibbs (1991); S. H. Holland, "Same Gender Classes in Baltimore: How to Avoid Problems Faced in Detroit, Milwaukee," *Journal of Equity and Excellence* 25(24) (1992): 93; S. M. Mancus, "Influence of Male Teachers on Elementary School Children's Stereotyping of Teacher Competence," *Sex Roles* 26(3) (1992): 112–15.

7. W. J. Wright, "The Endangered Black Male Child," *Educational Leadership* 49(4) (1992): 14–19.

8. V. LaPoint, "Accepting Community Responsibility for African American Youth Education and Socialization," *Journal of Negro Education* 6(4) (1992): 451–54.

9. W. C. Gill, "Jewish Day School and African-American Youth," *Journal of Higher Education* 60(4) (1991): 566–80.

10. Taylor (1997), 10, 21; J. Brown, "Coleman School's All-Male Class a Success," *Baltimore Sun*, June 12, 1991, D1–3; Gibbs (1991); P. G. Graham, "Black Teachers: A Drastically Scarce Resource," *Phi Delta Kappa* 68 (1987): 595–605.

11. D. Ruenzel, "War of Attrition," *Education Week* 18 (September, 1998): 33–35.

Chapter Three

Societal and Environmental Factors

Early prevention programs for at-risk children and their parents (starting with prenatal care and including health care, quality day care, and preschool education) help prevent debilitating educational efforts later. [1]

Impoverishment of a child's early environmental experiences, including any major restrictions on play activities or lack of feedback from older individuals, is suspected of slowing his/her social development and learning. The lack of adequate adult stimulation in the early years can lead to the development of negative social behavior, which may be irreversible. First, with the absence of adequate stimulation and activity, neurophysiological mechanisms involved in learning may fail to fully develop. Second, conditions in impoverished environments, where nourishment is a problem, generally do not provide a sufficient variety of opportunities for the child to develop their perceptual-motor skills to their fullest capacity. [2]

Children exposed to violent behavior can learn to be violent early. We need to start prior to the age of three years old and teach them more appropriate ways to handle frustration, and role-play the consequences of behavoirs and decisions for them.

HOME ENVIRONMENT

According to Butler,[3] children born into poverty and neglect often suffer from debilitating deprivations that seriously impair their ability to learn. Hamburg[4] indicated that early prevention programs for these at-risk children and their parents reduce educational problems during the school years.

Intervention in the earliest years is the most cost-effective way to improve the prospects of disadvantaged children. Early intervention programs should stress interpersonal relationships and tailored education programs.

Individuals are influenced by the elements within their environments. As a result, if we live in an environment that is a good match for our needs and abilities we will likely be more productive, be prone to stay, and will achieve academically. Individuals in mismatched environments, such as deprived environments that are poverty driven, often have trouble transferring values from one environment to another; therefore, many children leave school when they reach the legal age. All children, including black children, learn a great deal outside of the classroom. They have accomplished a vast amount of nonacademic learning before they enter school and continue to learn from both academic and nonacademic sources while they are enrolled. Historically, schools have not used the nonacademic learning resource as a viable one. Values, styles, and concepts that deprived black children bring to the schools must be matched and integrated into their own social reality if school experiences are to be meaningful.

Research reported by Erikson as early as 1959 supports the notion that environments characterized by mistrust, doubt, limitations, and feelings of inferiority and powerlessness contribute to identity confusion and inhibit the development of the mature individual.[5] In support of Erikson's view, Ayers[6] wrote that children need the home base of family life in order to grow up healthy and strong. They need to be listened to and understood, nurtured, and challenged by caring, committed adults. Parents need to contribute to their children's self-esteem, self-activity, or self-control through appropriate modeling strategies.

If a child's early development and early home environment are both low, there is an increased likelihood of poor developmental outcomes. The home environment is the foundation for further development within the child. Thus, it should be where the child receives support, experiences love, and acquires important skills toward becoming a productive, happy, social, and emotional person. Experiences from the home need to be integrated with the school curriculum for meaningful experiences to occur, which will necessitate including the family and the community in the education process.[7]

Many young African-American males live in substandard environments where they are denied appropriate mental, physical, and social stimulations. These conditions impede normal development in all areas of functioning. Consequently, direct and immediate intervention must be made in the social environment of these children if they are to profit sufficiently from their school experiences.

NOTES

1. K. Butler, "How Kids Learn: What Theorists Say," *Learning Styles* (1988): 30–34.

2. C. Dalli, "Scripts for Children's Lives: What Do Parents and Early Childhood Teachers Contribute to Children's Understanding of Events in their Lives?" (paper presented at fifth Early Childhood Convention, Dunedin, New Zealand, September 8–12, 1991), ERIC ED 344664 (1991); P. Dewitt, "The Crucial Early Years," *Time*, April 18, 1994, 16, 68.

3. Butler (1988).

4. D. A. Hamburg, *A Decent Start: Promoting Healthy Child Development in the First Three Years of Life* (Washington, DC: Clearinghouse on Teacher Education, 1992), ERIC ED 338431.

5. E. H. Erikson, "Identity and Life Cycle," *Psychological Issues, Monograph 1* (New York: International Universities Press, 1959).

6. W. Ayers, "Childhood at Risk," *Educational Leadership* 46(8) (1989): 70–72.

7. S. L. Kagan, "Early Care and Education: Beyond the Schoolhouse Doors," *Phi Delta Kappa* (1989): 107–12.

Chapter Four

Drug Education Awareness and Prevention Strategies

Collaboration between school, parents, and community is needed in order to plan a comprehensive drug curriculum. Community, student, and parental input ensure, to a larger extent, the success of the program. Collaborative efforts may be improved through formulating teams to set realistic goals, to identify physical and human resources, to assess the needs of the community, to develop a realistic and functional curriculum, to build an effective evaluation design that measures more than drug knowledge, and to change attitudes and behaviors of drug usage.[1]

Parental and community support are necessary for successful drug curricula. A first step may be to develop school-community teams. These stakeholders should be teachers, parents, students, local community agencies, businesses, and local, state, and federal agencies involved in drug prevention. A second step would be for the team to develop realistic objectives that impact drug use. A third step should involve the team conducting a need assessment in order to identify problems, the characteristics of the community, and human and physical resources.[2]

Questionnaires, surveys, and interviews may be used to gather information. Information of this nature is essential in developing an effective drug education program. A fourth step would be for the team to use the assessment data to develop a curriculum, which should be age appropriate, reveal symptoms of drug use, identify factors associated with dependency, include activities and strategies to reduce drug usage, show the social and cultural factors associated with drugs, and outline legal and medical aspects of drugs.[3] A fifth step for the team would be to develop an evaluation designed to measure the effectiveness of the curriculum.

The schools cannot be expected to rehabilitate youths in their neighborhoods and social environments. Sociologists and others who have worked in the drug abuse prevention field have pointed out that drug education is not a problem for the schools alone. It is a community problem and requires total community effort for its solution. The schools cannot assume the roles of parents, clergy, enforcement officers, physicians, or psychiatrists. But they can exercise leadership in facing a problem that the total community, working together, can try to remedy. This is education in its broadest and most important sense. It is making schools relevant to their communities. Schools should recognize the many positive contributions that parents and the community can contribute to drug education.[4]

An initial effort must be made to formulate school policies that are sensitive to the needs of all elements of the school community. There is no point, for example, in expecting "free" class discussions or adult cooperation when student informers are widely used throughout the school and teachers are required to report all suspected users to the police. If the school intends to act as an extension of civil authority, to investigate and turn users over to the police, it must come to terms with the fact that its effectiveness as an educational force will be substantially reduced. On the other hand, no school administrator can be expected to sit idly by while drug traffic flourishes within the school. Therefore, a major responsibility of school authorities is to give careful consideration to alternative choices in defining the school's action policy toward drug use. Once established, the policy should be clearly explained to students and their parents, as well as to the school staff.

The failure of school administrators to communicate with students about policies that they will be expected to obey inevitably creates mistrust of all official advice and information. By seeking and accepting input from young people and their parents in the formulation of school policies, school officials not only open up valuable channels of communication but make it possible to develop policies that are relevant to the needs, interests, and aspirations of each member of the school community.[5]

Dissatisfied with 2010 results, in 2011 many school systems tried a variety of new preventive-educational methods to discourage drug abuse, involving more direction by the students themselves.[6] The New York City Board of Education announced a trial program in sixteen high schools in which pupils designed and ran their own antidrug programs. In Philadelphia, selected students from seven high schools (accompanied by a teacher) learned basic drug facts from doctors, treatment experts, and law enforcement officials and went on field trips. They then went back to their own schools to initiate and run programs of their own choice. Most of them opened counseling services.

With regard to peer involvement, there are indications that students should be given a voice in basic approach, curriculum content, and choice of teachers, but should not be saddled with administrative chores, which they abhor and often perform poorly. Nevertheless, tapping the enthusiasm of well-selected students can be beneficial in motivating the student body to seek creative antidrug activities.[7] Students, parents, and community needs must be considered in planning a drug curriculum. Instruments should be designed to elicit from all stakeholders their attitudes toward the use of drugs and the danger of drugs. Results should be used to help construct a drug program based upon the above needs.

Peer group membership has a significant impact on youth taking drugs.[8] Youth may not accept drugs initially but rather share a cluster of values and beliefs that make substance abuse attractive. These values and beliefs will eventually lead the youth to taking drugs.[9] Stimmel's[10] findings support the above premise. He contends that drug-related behavior is strongly associated with drug experimentation among friends. Peer influence reaches its peak during early adolescence and manifests itself significantly with the use of marijuana and cigarette smoking.

The notion that young people relate to their peers better than to adults had validity but also limits. Young people relate to some of their peers. Rigid social groups exist in many schools, and students chosen by teachers and school officials may not be the best ones to lead the antidrug program to make it most effective. Whenever possible, some student participation in planning and operating programs should come from the group the program is trying to reach, whether nonusers, experimenters, or borderline cases. The student council in an Oregon high school sought the cooperation of ex-users and faculty in creating a youthful "Mod Squad." Teams of experienced students provided successful peer counseling, assistance in crisis situations, and referrals to local treatment facilities and otherwise contributed positively to the school's educational programming. In developing goals, goal 6 of the National Goals for Education should be consulted.

Goal 6 of the National Goals for Education of 1990 focused on safe, disciplined, and drug-free schools. This goal stated that by the year 2000, every school in America will be free of drugs and violence and would offer a disciplined environment conducive to learning. Many attempts have been made to achieve this goal. Several school districts have experimented with comprehensive drug prevention programs. In some instances, programs have been infused with health and physical education programs; in other instances, separate drug prevention programs have been developed.

Collective data from these studies have clearly shown in 2002 that goal 6 has not been achieved. In a recent survey, 19 percent of high-school seniors indicated that they had smoked cigarettes, and 9 percent had drunk alcohol by sixth grade; half of eighth graders had smoked cigarettes, 77 percent reported having used alcohol, and slightly over half of twelfth graders reported at least one experience with illicit drugs. This experience may lead to youth being exposed to dangerous conditions. The infusion of drug education should be integrated into specific content areas.

In order to move forward to achieve the goals articulated over the last decade, school systems and districts must have well-developed plans consisting of: (1) assessing and identifying prevention strategies based upon the uniqueness of the community; (2) providing in-service training for all stakeholders; (3) incorporating parents' and the community's participation in developing and implementing, coordinating, adopting, and modifying the program as evaluative results indicate; and (4) identifying funding sources. Achieving goals and developing programs can be expensive. Educators must implement a strategic plan for financial assistance.

FAMILY-SCHOOL COLLABORATION

Children who use drugs have a negative impact on the total family. Some spouses are unable to tolerate the behaviors displayed by their children using drugs. Siblings are also affected. They may attempt to model behaviors of their parents or siblings. Children may consume alcohol because they observe a parent drinking or taking drugs, such as their mothers taking diet pills, or they may resort to selling drugs to reduce financial difficulties at home.

Additionally, research has shown that a family void of religious principles may result in depression and apathy on the part of the children. Lack of spiritual foundation may lead to a negative, do-not-care attitude, which might promote drug usage. Other researchers have voiced that parents have a significant impact on their children's decisions to use drugs. They may reduce this exposure by monitoring their children's activities, questioning strange behaviors, and noting the type of friendships their children develop.

In support of the above view, Jones articulated that an essential component of an effective drug program is parental and community involvement and that all parents have information which can make the program successful. The school may tap this widely used source by encouraging family unity and support. Domino and Carroll[11] wrote that this type of unity may satisfy the need of youths who might otherwise be driven to gang involvement and membership.

ROLE OF THE COMMUNITY

It would be indicative of gross neglect not to explore the role and dimensions of the community in problem solving. A desirable relationship between school, home, and community is one that is marked by a strong bond of understanding and cooperation between parents and school personnel. Parents should have a direct share in deciding what problem-solving techniques appear to service their children best. Parents should be welcome to make suggestions for the guidance of their children. Through various channels, the school can improve collaboration for children with various needs, including disability related needs, in cooperation with parent and community involvement.

It has been commonly stated that no effective program can operate successfully for children with disabilities unless there is a common understanding between various segments of the community and the parents. All necessary information concerning the education of the child should be collaborated with the parent. Parents and the community should have direct input into the development of a program. For teachers and related school personnel, collaboration should involve the utilization of information from parents and community to develop instructional programs.

Several authors all concurred that effective collaboration implies more than simply establishing links with the home; rather it requires a comprehensive and permanent program of partnership with families and communities. Marsh summarized some of the values of partnership or collaboration between the home, the community, and the school. Effective partnerships or collaboration can improve

1. school climate and programs;
2. family support services;
3. parents' skills and leadership;
4. family and community relationships;
5. teacher effectiveness.

COLLABORATIVE PLANNING

Research by Thompson clearly indicates that gaining public and professional support for the school involves developing strategies that incorporate widespread participation in the development of standards by stakeholders. Some of the strategies could be designed to assist teachers in drafting district-wide standards.

Parental leadership skill workshops should be instituted to enable parents to become active participants in developing standards and educational decisions. Stakeholders who develop standards must share mutual commitments and responsibilities. Before enacting standards, the wider community should be informed and give its endorsement. The school must show concern and respect for all participants, regardless of class, education, or diversity. This approach assures that democratic views and values are considered in educational planning.

Collaborative planning should be more than mere discussions and suggestions given by stakeholders. Rather, stakeholders should be engaged in developing strategies to bring about educational reforms and changes. Research findings tend to support that home-to-school collaboration is essential to the academic success of students. Collaborative arrangements increase parental decision making and provide opportunities for school personnel to support parents in assisting their children to learn. Parents who have a conceptual understanding of the subject matter taught can better assist the child and augment the teacher's teaching strategies.

A unique way for improving parent-teacher collaboration is to develop teams consisting of both parents and teachers. Miller offered the following suggestions for improving parent-teacher teams:

1. Be in touch long before the conference.
2. Be direct and personal in arranging the conference.
3. Be accommodating and try not to take no for an answer. Be flexible in setting meeting times around parents' schedules.
4. Be on time.
5. Be prepared with handouts and work samples.
6. Be specific about problems.
7. Be knowledgeable as a team about each student.
8. Be welcoming.
9. Be in charge.
10. Be supportive.
11. Consider student-led conferences, which can be very effective for positive home-school relations.
12. Follow up. Hold a team meeting to develop strategies for following up recommendations from the team and to assign duties and responsibilities.

Team interaction is an important essential for improving the education of children with disabilities. This interaction can better assist the team in understanding the strengths and weaknesses of the child under study. The team may also act as an advocate for the disabled child and assure that significant support is available to enable the disabled child to achieve his or her stated objectives.

MODEL PROGRAMS FOR IMPROVING COLLABORATION

Lewis and Morris reported on two successful programs involving parents working in the schools, the Charlotte-Mecklenburg, North Carolina, and El Paso, Texas, public schools. Koerner[12] also reported on a successful collaborative program in Cobb County, Georgia. Thousands, many of whom were parents, volunteered to work in the schools in these school districts. Volunteers served as teachers, mentors, lunch aides, lecturers, instructors in academic subjects, as coaches for games, and in a variety of other services designed by the schools. Social events were also held to unify parents, teachers, and administrators. In addition, parental involvement included conducting mediation sessions and implementing conflict resolution strategies, donating goods and services, staffing the schools' administrative offices, and serving on advisory boards.

Another innovative approach to parental involvement is rating teachers. Some teachers may be threatened by this process, but research by Rich has shown that parental ratings can introduce new concepts and ideas by providing innovative strategies to educate their children as well as to provide the basis for ongoing discussions relevant to curriculum modification. Parents rated teachers on the following:

1. enjoying teaching;
2. setting high expectations for children and assisting children in reaching them;
3. demonstrating competency in the subject matter taught;
4. creating a productive and safe environment for children to learn in;
5. utilizing effective strategies for dealing with behavior problems in a fair and just way;
6. assigning meaningful homework assignments;
7. understanding the principles of childhood development;
8. using a variety of communicating tools to report students' progress and needs.

Parental involvement in collaborative efforts with the school should not be imposed upon parents by the school. Parents must feel motivated and competent in any involvement. They should have the right to choose not to be involved when they feel that it is not in their best interest, that their involvement will not benefit their children, or that they do not have the competencies to perform the assigned tasks. In essence, the degree of parental participation should be determined by the parents' needs and interests, not by some predetermined standards set by educators. A model for collaboration is presented to assist parents, educators, and the community in developing an effective collaborative plan. The aforementioned models project collaborative planning at its best.

A MODEL FOR PARENT-TEACHER COMMUNICATION

It has been projected throughout this chapter that a systematic plan was needed to develop a collaboration plan. The model appears to be one technique to develop a system-wide plan. The model is an attempt to visually be used in collaborative planning. According to Shea and Bauer, their model is essentially a prescriptive-teaching methodology. Activities emphasize exclusively positive, human child-raising practice and behavior-management techniques that recognize each parent and child as an individual with unique abilities, needs, and environmental influences.

Implementation of the Shea and Bauer model can provide a format for developing a realistic model for collaboration and infusing, integrating, and respecting individual ideas. Additionally, the model will provide a mechanism whereby communication can be expedited and strategies included to improve interpersonal skills. Interpersonal skills training is needed by both teachers and parents. Since teachers are the professionals, they should be aware of interpersonal skills, which will promote rather than retard communication in conferring with parents.

CONFERRING WITH PARENTS

Parents may request a conference concerning their children for a variety of reasons. Teachers may feel apprehensive about the conference, but they should realize that like themselves, parents also want their children to be successful and thus view the conference as an opportunity to improve the educational opportunities for children, including those with disabilities. McLaughlin wrote that, frequently, teachers are not prepared in their training to conduct conferences and must learn on the job.

Parents also need to make preparations for attending a conference. According to Kines, the following preparations are recommended:

1. Prepare a list of topics to discuss.

2. Involve the child if possible in a three-way conference.
3. Be on time. It is unfair to keep others waiting; parents and teachers have busy schedules.
4. Come right to the point. Clarify points to be discussed.
5. Ask about class participation of the child.
6. Request clarification on any issue not fully understood.
7. Ask to see the child's work samples.
8. Talk about your child outside of school in order to inform the teacher of community and other out-of-school activities.
9. Stay within the time limit. If additional time is needed, schedule another meeting or a telephone conference.
10. Write a note of appreciation to the teacher, indicating the many positive things he or she has done to improve skills for the child. This note can indicate an agenda for the next meeting as well.

Communication and collaboration are essential for teachers and parents if children with disabilities are to profit sufficiently from their educational experiences. Some recommended strategies for teachers to improve in communication and collaboration, according to Perl, are

1. building rapport—establish the dignity and worth of the parent's contribution at the outset;
2. listening—learn to listen actively to the parent; be attentive to responses;
3. expressing empathy—be aware of the nature and type of responses made by the parent; put yourself in the parent's place;
4. reflecting affect—attempt to reflect how the parent feels; show empathy at the appropriate times;
5. clarifying statements—restate the point by saying "do you mean" or "are you inferring" in regard to a particular statement.

Parent-teacher conferences can serve useful purposes and provide invaluable information to improve the child's academic program. Consequently, both parents and teachers must take a positive approach. The first step is to improve the quality of communication. Carefully planned group and individual conferences are initial ways to improve communication. A successful group conference can set the tone for the year and build a strong rapport between teachers and parents.

PARENTAL VIEWS

Parental views toward inclusion are important. Parental reactions toward having their children placed in inclusive or segregated classrooms parallel the views of advocates and opponents of the measurement, which is multidimensional. In essence, parental perceptions support the statement that inclusion is no panacea for educating all of their disabled children. Their perceptions vacillate greatly between inclusion and special education placement.

The disability is not the major reason why some parents do not want their children in inclusive settings. Issues such as instructional objectives, competent personnel, instructional strategies, delivery models, resources, and related services take precedent over placement, because the issue of parental involvement is so critical to the inclusion process. Inclusion cannot be successfully achieved until the school and parents collaboratively develop strategies concerning inclusion. School personnel must be trained to demonstrate competencies in conferencing skills and must be well informed about the problems parents face as a result of having disabled children.

As indicated, many of the studies reported dealt with mainstreaming rather than inclusion, did not designate the type of disabilities being accessed, and mostly focused on children with mild or moderate disabilities. According to Taylor, suggestions to improve results concerning the efficacy of inclusion with segregation will necessitate developing a comprehensive evaluation model—one that investigates all skill areas affected by the disability. Multiple means of collecting information should be used (e.g., observations, interviews, standardized instruments, and alternative approaches).

SCHOOL AND COMMUNITY INTERACTIONS

Research has shown that community involvement and action can be powerful allies in transforming schools. Community involvement with the schools has been credited with (1) improving the physical conditions and resources that support learning in the schools, (2) raising the attitudes and expectations of parents, teachers, and students, and (3) improving the depth and quality of the learning experiences of students through collaborative planning.[13] The major purpose of school/community relations is to share information about the special education program.

It is essential that educators make parents aware and informed about progress made toward achieving reforms. Parents are more likely to become associated with the school if educators develop a strong and trusting relationship with them. The bond can be further strengthened by making frequent contacts with the parents, conducting seminars, and sponsoring social events developed by the community. Educators frequently deal with community groups and agencies and must possess effective interpersonal and community skills.

Because of the emotional impact of disability upon the family, parents need help from the community. Services provided by the community impact, to some degree, how children with or without disabilities develop, and can also provide strategies to help family members cope with their children. The community's most important contribution to families is a willingness to listen and understand what they are experiencing. Parents and siblings need someone they can express their feelings to and receive support from. Educators can ensure that parents' needs are heard through school/community relations designed to share information about special education with the community.

The need for direct involvement of parents and communities has been advocated by Atkinson and Juntunen. They reported that educators must function as a school-home-community liaison. Casas and Furlong supported the increase of parental participation and empowerment in the community and encouraged parents to visit with other parents of children with disabilities. Most communities have support groups of parents who have disabled children. Organizations dealing with the specific disability of the child can also be helpful to the family (e.g., the Association of Retarded Citizens, United Cerebral Palsy Association).

According to Lunenburg and Ornstein, educators can use the following ideas to keep parents and the community informed:

- a brochure that describes the education/special education program, including the district's philosophy of services to individuals with disabilities;
- specialized brochures, each describing a specific aspect of the program;
- a parent handbook that describes the IEP process, forms, and the role of the parent;
- articles in the district newspaper, school building paper, or local newspaper;
- a special newsletter that focuses on special/education news;
- telephone contacts with individual parents and other citizens;
- speeches to community groups or civic clubs;
- annual reports, open houses, videotapes, and letters to groups;
- displays at locations, such as civic meeting places and shopping malls;
- public service announcements on radio and television describing some aspect of special/education services.

Collaboration strategies can also be used effectively to promote communication.

Collaborative activities can meet the needs of children, including those with disabilities, and their parents by integrating the services of both the home and school in all areas of human functioning. These activities may do much to improve cultural, social, and physical problems associated with the children's needs. Educators must strive to become an integral part of the collaborative efforts if they are to be successful. The following guidelines are offered as a means to improve the collaborative efforts:

1. Develop a plan to build trust and security among parents.
2. Involve parents in the school development plan and seek volunteers in all aspects of the plan to ensure that every parent contributes to the attainment of the goals and objectives.
3. Construct individual agreements with each parent so that the parent will have some responsibilities in meeting the stated goals, objectives, and IEP requirements.
4. Establish a citizen advisory committee and involve it in the planning.

Several authors have indicated disadvantages in promoting collaborative activities, especially advisory committees.

1. Advisory committees can consume a great deal of the administrator's time.
2. Committee members often lack perspective and background information about educational issues.
3. Special interests of individual committee members can dominate.
4. Committee members may not be aware of past school practices or how the school operates.
5. Committee members may not understand group dynamics or group decision-making procedures.
6. Final recommendations can exceed the committee's original charge or overstep its authority.
7. The committee may search for problems or issues to justify its existence.

We believe educators can overcome many of the pitfalls just listed by developing small focus groups who are knowledgeable about the issues under discussion and are willing to reach a consensus. Members of this group should have time to commit to the issues. Additionally, educators should apprise the group of any history or procedures that will assist them in reaching a consensus, provide as much assistance as possible to the group, and implement as many of the committee's recommendations as possible. Lack of implementing the committee's recommendations will erode the relationship between the committee and administrators.

Collaborating with parents and working with families are major modifications and reforms that educators can make in improving communication between the home and school. Much of the improvement in communication has come about due mainly to state and federal legislation, parental rights groups, parent empowerment, and the schools' recognition of the value of parental input in educating children. Educators have become cognizant of the influence of poverty, ethnicity, family structure and transitions, parental age, and other factors that interact with children's development. Using the vast amount of research generated in these areas, educators have developed programs to strengthen parental behaviors as well as revised programs to reflect cultural diversity.

PROMOTING CULTURAL AWARENESS

Promoting cultural awareness helps families with different cultural and linguistic backgrounds, including children with disabilities, to participate fully in the schools. Variables such as socioeconomic status, educational level, and length of residence in the country should not promote stereotyped beliefs. Hyun and Fowler explored how cultural awareness can be enhanced by exploring one's own cultural heritage and examining the attitudes and behaviors associated with one's own culture. Educators must become familiar with the child's culture and community. [14]

COMMUNITY AND PARENTAL INVOLVEMENT

No school program can be completely effective without the support of parents and the community. Most educators are acutely aware of the need for parents' and active community involvement in the entire educational program for children. When the school and community are genuinely interested in the welfare of the child and his or her parents, apathy and despair turn to hope and self-fulfillment, which can do much to ease many of the emotional problems experienced. Further, improvement in communication can do much to eliminate the negativism of many parents. This positive approach cannot help but assist the child, especially the child with a disability, in his or her educational pursuits.

A desirable relationship in the community is one marked by a strong bond of understanding and cooperation between parents and school personnel. Parents should have a direct share in deciding what types of instruction appear to serve their children best. Parents should be welcome to make suggestions for the guidance of their children. Through various channels the educator should enlist the cooperation of parents and community agencies in designing and implementing educational programs for all children. In communities where educators work with parents and with religious, recreational, and social agencies in a constructive effort to help, the results are reflected in healthier personalities of boys and girls.

Communities can do a great deal to make better use of their resources through a collaboration of efforts. Coordination mobilizes the skills of people to help all programs, eliminates wasteful competition, saves money, improves training opportunities, and gives invaluable assistance to all children in need and his or her family. The school should be the key for coordinating activities in the community. Specialists in various disciplines should be consulted as the needs of all children, particularly disabled children, dictate. Some consideration should be given to any parents who may need financial assistance. Again, personnel in the schools and diagnostic centers can refer the parents to appropriate community agencies that can provide the support.

Differentiation of general and specialized services is vital, not only to make ample use of community resources but to provide the disabled child, in particular, with a complete diagnosis. Services provided should include both approaches. Coordinated planning should be a well-planned process that seeks to elicit cooperation and communication among various community agencies. Some of the obstacles associated with effective community planning are (1) lack of personnel with experience to conduct the planning, (2) decreased interdisciplinary communication due to lack of mutual respect among specialists, (3) facilities for the disabled failing to recognize that no one clinic or agency can provide the necessary services needed to diagnose, treat, and rehabilitate the disabled child, and (4) exclusion of parents from the initial diagnostic evaluation, treatment, and follow-up procedure.

The position of school personnel on a special education team headed by noneducators and the relationship of medical personnel with other members are some specific problems that should not vary as widely as they do from program to program. Understanding the intricacies of teamwork and agreeing upon its definition might clarify areas of misunderstanding. The necessity of communication within the team, or team action with parents, community members, state departments, and other programs, as well as balancing progress, morals, and democratic ideals, constitute other areas of coordination sometimes overlooked by administrators.

STRATEGIES FOR IMPROVING PARENTAL INVOLVEMENT

Much of the interest and increase in parental involvement may be attributed to P.L. 94-142, the Education for All Handicapped Children Act, and its amendments. These legislative amendments have mandated parental participation in all aspects of the child's educational program, including assessment, IEP (Individualized Education Program) development, placement decisions, evaluation, follow-up, and transitional services.

REWARDING PARENTS

Educators need to recognize and reward parents for their involvement. Reinforcing parental efforts can make a significant impact in working with their children. Parents employ some of the same techniques that teachers use to reinforce their children. Social and academic growth of children may be expedited through the use of reinforcement strategies. Teachers who create a positive atmosphere for communication and collaboration with parents increase the probability of the child's success in his or her academic pursuits.

Many parents are not trained in teaching strategies. School personnel can train interested parents through observation, demonstration, and modeling. Bandura has validated the importance of these techniques. School personnel should provide ample strategies for parents to imitate. Today, school personnel realize the importance of parental involvement and understand that cooperative efforts between teachers and parents benefit the children significantly.

NOTES

1. D. J. Layne and D. R. Grossnickle, "A Teamwork Approach to the Prevention of Chemical Abuse and Dependency," *NASSP Bulletin* 73(514) (1989): 98–101.

2. R. Lewis and J. Morris, "Communities for Children," *Educational Leadership* (1998): 34–36.

3. G. R. Taylor, *Practical Application of Social Learning Theories in Educating Young African-American Males* (Lanham, MD: University Press of America, 2003).

4. J. Hyum and S. A. Fowler, "Respect, Cultural Sensitivity, and Communication," *Teaching Exceptional Children* 28(1) (1995): 25–28.

5. A. Bandura, *A Social Learning Theory* (Englewood Cliffs, NJ: Prentice-Hall, 1997).

6. J. H. Palmer and C. L. Ringwalt, "Prevalence of Alcohol and Drug Use among North Carolina Public School Students," *Journal of School Health* 58(7) (September 1988): 288–91; J. P. McGovern and R. L. DuPont, "Student Assistance Programs: An Important Approach to Drug Abuse Prevention," *Journal of School Health* 61(6) (1991): 260–64.

7. S. Moore, "Piaget and Bandura: The Need for a Unified Theory of Learning" (paper presented at the biannual meeting of the Society for Research in Child Development, Baltimore, MD, April 23–26, 1987); K. Nelson-Simley and L. Erickson, "The Nebraska 'Network of Drug-Free Youth' Program," *Journal of School Health* 65 (1995): 49–53.

8. K. I. Klepp, A. Halper, and C. L. Perry, "The Efficacy of Peer Leaders in Drug Abuse Prevention," *Journal of School Health* 56 (1986): 407–11.

9. N. S. Mounts and L. Steinberg, "An Ecological Analysis of Peer Influence on Adolescent Grade Point Average and Drug Use," *Developmental Psychology* 31 (1995): 915–22.

10. D. J. Layne and D. R. Grossnickle, "A Teamwork Approach to the Prevention of Chemical Abuse and Dependency," *NASSP Bulletin* 73(514) (1989): 98–101.

11. R. Lewis and J. Morris, "Communities for Children," *Educational Leadership* (1998): 34–36.

12. Taylor (2003).

13. Hyum and Fowler (1995).

14. Bandura (1997).

Chapter Five

Modeling Themes for Parental Support

Parents may employ principles of social cognitive theories in developing appropriate social skills with African-American males through using modeling, observation, imitation, and rewarding individuals for appropriate behaviors. Singly or combined, these principles have been successfully used to decrease maladaptive behaviors of individuals. There is a body of research confirming that this is true for African-American males. Parents may use strategies in this theory to model and teach the boys acceptable ways of dealing with internalizing and controlling their behaviors. The consequences of the boys not controlling their behavior may result in their demonstrating inappropriate behaviors. Educators should provide parents with strategies on how the boys can internalize their behaviors by thinking before they act and not submitting to peer pressure.

Social cognitive principles can also aid parents in motivating and in preventing low self-esteem of the boys. It is important that parents recognize that when the boys are motivated, they present fewer behavioral problems; therefore, parents should be instructed by the school in the use of various forms of motivational strategies such as believing in oneself, establishing functional and realistic rules and consequences, giving frequent praise and rewards, offering less criticism, accenting interests, and identifying and eliminating factors associated with negative behaviors.

THEORETICAL FRAMEWORK

The major emphasis of social learning and cognitive theories is on environmental learner interaction. The learning behaviors that are socially accepted, as well as those that are not, are "social learning." This view is supported by

Stuart,[1] who maintained that social learning theories attempt to describe the process by which we come to know what behaviors should be or should not be projected when we are in different types of social situations.

The theories themselves are learning theories that have been applied to social situations. Generally, they have been behavioristic rather than cognitive.[2] These theories do not separate the parts from the whole; instead, they have as a major underlying concept the holistic and interactive nature of development. For example, the various areas of the self do not exist or develop separately from one another, and movement toward maturity in one area can affect movement and learning in another area. Social learning theories also address individual differences and how such factors as personality, temperament, and sociological influences may interact with the developmental process.

Learning theories assist parents in identifying how different individuals may manage, delay, progress through, or retreat from developmental tasks. These theories also suggest that there are persistent individual differences such as cognitive style, temperament, or ethnic background that interact with development. Additionally, these theories provide knowledge about individual types and styles that may be critical to our understanding of differing sources of reward and punishment for students.[3]

One of the major tenets of the theories is that there is a functional relationship between the effects of the culture and cognitive development and biological growth. Whereas the physical and neurological determinants are more readily understood and agreed upon, the impact of the cultural determinants is not easily understood. Cultural determinants include social processes which transform naturally through the mastery and use of culture signs. Culture provides the conditions by which the higher psychological processes may be realized.[4] These tenets may be responsible for inappropriate behaviors if not addressed by parents. Parents must instruct their boys in the differences between social norms in both cultures.

COMMONALITY AMONG THEORIES

The common threads uniting these theories and concepts are imitation, modeling, and copying behaviors.[5] As do all children, African-American males imitate, model, and copy behaviors directly from their environments. Too often these models are inappropriate and often create conflict and tension between children, society, and the school. Therefore, learning, culture, and behavioral styles of African-American males should be, as much as possible, incorporated and integrated. Social learning theories provide a concrete framework to begin implementing additional social skills strategies.

"Social skills" is a term used to describe a wide range of behaviors varying in complexity and is thought to be necessary for effective functioning and academic success.[6] Behaviors that constitute social skills development may vary depending upon the situation, role, sex, age, and culture values.

INTEGRATIVE ASPECTS OF SOCIAL SKILLS DEVELOPMENT

Various types of social skills instruction must be developed and systematically taught to African-American males. The earlier the intervention, the sooner negative behaviors can be addressed. The parents should play dominant roles in developing prosocial skills due to several factors associated with the urban environment.

Teachers are the most appropriate individuals to conduct the social skills training or intervention. Teaching students prosocial skills necessary to cope with the social demands of society creates a climate in which positive relationships can exist and where the boys can be empowered to direct their own successes.

Parents may develop social skills through interactions with family, school, and community, and they are shaped by reinforcement received as a result of such interactions. Often children do not learn effectively from past experiences. Frequently, they are enabled to transfer one socially accepted behavior to another social situation; thus, their behaviors are frequently interpreted as immature, inept, or intrusive. This negative feedback prohibits future social interactions. This is especially true for African-American males.

Research findings suggest a significant relationship between social skills intervention and academic achievement. Thus, many social skill procedures, such as attention and positive interaction techniques, have been shown to increase academic performance. According to Oswald and Singh,[7] social skills interventions appear to work best when they correspond to actual interactions in the natural environment.

Social norms in the natural environment are frequently different from norms in the largest environment, which are based and established on laws. Conflicts in behavioral standards frequently exist because of this conflict. The degree and nature of the conflicts may lead to activities which may be assessed as criminal activities.

Lack of appropriate social training may be an impediment for many African-American males to engage productively in social events. Findings by Lloyd[8] stated that young African-American males began to slide academically before the third or fourth grade. Special techniques and interventions related to remediating poor or inappropriate skills must be addressed early in their school experiences in order to bring their social skills up to acceptable school standards. According to Ayers,[9] early intervention is needed to expose young black males to appropriate social models.

For many African-American males, culture experiences have not provided appropriate social skills for them to be successful in the larger community or to cope with appropriate social behavior. Parents can assist in changing inappropriate social behavior of boys by infusing principles of social learning theories such as modeling, imitation, and behavioral techniques with social skills instruction. Once the social skill deficits have been identified, the social learning principles may be used to reinforce or reward appropriate social behavior. It is recommended that educators and the schools provide training for parents in social skills strategies as well.

SOCIAL SKILLS MODELS OF YOUNG AFRICAN-AMERICAN MALES

Research findings have demonstrated that diverse groups of children, such as young black males, are at risk for developing inappropriate interpersonal skills. Several factors, such as child-rearing practices, deprived cultural environments, and lack of understanding of social expectations or rules, may attribute to these deficiencies. In turn, such deficiencies may lead to inappropriate or inadequate social behaviors.

Since social skills are learned throughout a lifetime from imitating or modeling both negative and positive behaviors, many individuals lack basic interpersonal skills if deprived of appropriate models. These individuals are frequently at a disadvantage in society and tend to feel inadequate and use unproductive and unacceptable ways of relating to and communicating with others.

Mastering these skills requires training and practice. Interpersonal skills training allows children to recognize appropriate social behaviors, to understand individual's responses to certain behaviors, and to respond appropriately. Lack of these skills often leads to feelings of rejection and isolation in any public setting.

TEACHING ANGER AND HOSTILITY CONTROL

Studies have consistently shown that negative behaviors such as anger and hostility are learned behaviors that children imitate from their environments. Parents should be trained by the school and other community agencies to assist them in intervention techniques. These behaviors manifest themselves in hostile and destructive patterns of behavior, which frequently cannot be controlled if not addressed during the early years.

Controlling anger and managing feelings are essential in developing appropriate interpersonal skills. Parents should teach children how to control anger by using the following application:

1. recognizing and describing anger;
2. finding appropriate ways to express anger;
3. analyzing and understanding factors responsible for anger;
4. managing anger by looking at events differently or talking oneself out of anger;
5. learning how to repress feelings;
6. expressing anger constructively;
7. experimenting with alternative ways of expressing anger.

A variety of strategies may be used by parents to assist African-American males in controlling or reducing anger. Role playing, creative dramatics, physical activities, time-out, relaxation therapy, writing and talking out feelings, assertive behavioral techniques, managing provocations activities, and resolving interpersonal conflicts through cooperative approaches are but a few techniques that parents may employ. As indicated, parents may need to be trained by community agencies in the above techniques.

TEACHING APOLOGY STRATEGIES

Apologies can restore relationships, heal humiliations, and generate forgiveness if taught appropriately. Apologizing is a powerful social skill that should be taught by the parents in collaboration with the school. This is especially true for a significant number of African-American males, many of whom consider apologies to be signs of weakness, displays of feminine traits, and admissions of failure. Parents must teach and model the importance of apology strategies. The few research studies reported indicated the reverse: apologies require great strength, empathy, security, and strength.

In this chapter, specific strategies have been outlined for parents to teach most social skills to African-American males. Some African-American males have observed anger and hostility, and they need to be taught apology strategies.

Harris concluded that many African-American males may have developed or adapted alternative ways and styles of coping with problems in their neighborhoods. These behavioral styles are frequently in conflict with the school and society in general and may be viewed as negative or destructive. Behavioral styles and models copied and imitated by African-American males may serve them well in their environments but are frequently viewed as dysfunctional by the school and society, which may lead to criminal acts and incarcerations.

TEACHING SELF-REGULATION SKILLS

Programs must be developed by parents in conjunction with the school and designed to enable African-American males to gain knowledge about appropriate interpersonal skills and to employ this newly acquired knowledge in solving their social problems. For this goal to be accomplished, these boys must be taught effective ways of internalizing their behaviors and assessing how their behaviors affect others. Helping African-American males develop self-regulation skills appears to be an excellent technique for bringing behaviors to the conscious level, where they can be controlled. Some of the more commonly used self-regulation skills that parents can implement in teaching interpersonal skills which may reduce maladaptive behaviors in the future are summarized by Taylor as follows.

BE AWARE OF ONE'S THINKING PATTERNS

Provide "think-aloud" activities and model how to solve problems by working through tasks and asking questions such as (1) What is needed to solve the problem? (2) Things are not working out; should I try another way? and (3) What assistance do I need to solve the problem?

As parents perform these think-aloud activities, they may ask for input from the student relevant to the type of self-regulation skills being demonstrated. Skills may have to be modeled and demonstrated several times; provide opportunities for the boys to demonstrate them individually and in cooperative groups, as well as to evaluate the effectiveness of their actions.

MAKING A PLAN

Have the boys identify specific examples where self-regulation is useful. Motivation may come from a story, file, tape, or creative dramatic activities. Instruct the boys to develop a plan to reduce, correct, or eliminate the undesirable behaviors. As the boys demonstrate the behaviors, the parent should reinforce and praise them.

DEVELOP AND EVALUATE LONG-TERM GOALS

Employ self-regulation strategies to assist the boys in accomplishing long-term goals. First have the boys identify social and behavioral goals. Record these goals and assist the boys in making a plan, as outlined previously. Schedule a time to meet with the boys to determine how well the goals are being achieved. In some instances, the goals will need to be modified or adapted such that they focus on specific behaviors. Self-regulation strategies make actions more controllable by making us aware of our own behavior. Once awareness is achieved, the plan outlined earlier may be taught to bring behaviors under control.

A variety of techniques and strategies may be used in developing self-regulation skills: (1) role playing; (2) classifying behaviors and identifying types of self-regulation strategies to employ; (3) working in cooperative groups; (4) positively reinforcing the mental habits; (5) reading and developing stories; (6) being sensitive to feedback and criticism; (7) teaching self-monitoring skills; (8) seeking outside advice when needed; and (9) evaluating progress.

Self-regulation is one of several strategies that may be used to teach appropriate social skills to African-American males. Appropriate social skills are essential for developing personal relationships and accepting the roles of authority figures. Since social behaviors are learned, they can be changed and modified with appropriate intervention. They require that an individual evaluate the situation, choose the appropriate skills, and perform the social tasks appropriately. Unfortunately, many African-American males have not been exposed to appropriate social models or do not possess enough prerequisite skills, such as maturity and self-control, to successfully perform the social skills. As mentioned, the development of social skills in African-American males, as well as in all children, requires that they have appropriate models to copy and imitate, that they can recognize nonverbal clues, and that they adjust their behaviors accordingly.

Several researchers have supported the value of social skills in developing positive behaviors. Findings from other studies support these studies by concluding that many African-American males may have developed or adapted alternative ways and styles of coping with problems within their communities, which are frequently in conflict with the school and society in general and, therefore, are viewed as negative or destructive.

SUMMARY

Social learning theories offer parents a common context through which African-American males' environment, developmental sequence, and early experiences can be understood and researched. Thus, these theories enable parents to better understand how African-American males think and feel about themselves, thereby making them aware of factors in the environment that precipitate cognitive and affective problems that may have some bearing on academic performance.

Cognitive learning has led to improving our understanding of the social nature of learning, the importance of context on understanding, the need for domain-specific knowledge in higher-order thinking, expert-novice differences in thinking and problem solving, and the belief that learners can be instructed to construct their own understanding of a topic. Variables such as drives, habits, and strengths play critical roles in learning. Learning is developmental, and children must master each task before mastering advanced tasks. Learning is facilitated by the boy's acquisition of new skills and experiences. How the boys interpret and receive information can accelerate or impede learning. Identifying and assessing learning styles are important in evaluating achievement.

The relationship between social learning theories and academic performance is not well established. Most research reported today simply indicates a causal relationship. There is a dire need to conduct empirical studies to determine to what degree social learning theories impact academic performance.

Social development is a major area in which many African-American males need assistance, since they frequently have developed inappropriate interpersonal skills that are not accepted by society. The inability to conform to expected social standards may result in a lack of social skills that are essential for developing personal relationships and accepting the role of authority figures. Research findings support the notion that unacceptable behaviors are directly associated with deprived cultural environments. Innovative ways must be found to provide appropriate role models for African-American males to imitate and copy. Applying the social skills techniques provided in this chapter will assist in reducing the incarceration rates of African-American males between eighteen and thirty-five in the criminal justice system.

NOTES

1. A. G. Hilliard, "Teachers and Culture Styles in a Pluralist Society," *NEA Today* 7(6) (1989): 65–69; K. Butler, "How Kids Learn: What Theorists Say," *Learning Styles* (1989): 30–34; S. H. Holland, "A Radical Approach to Educating Black Males," *Education Week Commentary* (1987): 24–25; W. Johnson and R. Johnson, "Social Skills for Successful Group Work," *Educational Leadership* 47(4) (1990): 29–33.

2. A. Bandura, *A Social Learning Theory* (Englewood Cliffs, NJ: Prentice-Hall, 1977).

3. R. B. Stuart, "Social Learning Theory: A Vanishing or Expanding Presence?" *Psychology: A Journal of Human Behavior* 26(1) (1989): 15–26.

4. I. Moll, "The Material and Social in Vygotsky's Theory of Cognitive Development" (paper presented at the biennial meeting of the Society for Research in Child Development, Seattle, WA, April 18–21, 1991), ERIC ED 352186.

5. A. Bandura and R. Walters, *Social Learning and Personality Development* (New York: Holt, Rinehart and Winston, 1963).

6. F. E. Obiakor, "Development of Self-Concept: Impact of Student's Learning," *Journal of the Southeastern Association of Educational Opportunity Program Personnel* 9(1) (1990): 16–33.

7. D. P. Oswald and N. Singh, "Current Research on Social Behavior," *Behavior Modification* 16(4) (1992): 443–47.

8. D. N. Lloyd, "Prediction of School Failure from Third Grade Data," *Educational and Psychological Measurement* 38(4) (1978): 193–200.

9. G. R. Taylor, "Impact of Social Learning Theory on Educating Deprived/Minority Children," Clearinghouse for Teacher Education (Washington, DC: ERIC ED 349260, 1992); G. R. Taylor, *Black Male Project* (report submitted to Sinclair Lane Elementary School, Baltimore, MD, 1993).

Chapter Six

Learning Theories for Parents

Social learning theories offer parents a common context in which the environment, developmental sequence, and early experiences of African-American males can be understood and researched. These theories enable parents to better understand how these children think and how they feel about themselves. They also make parents more aware of factors in the environment that precipitate cognitive and affective problems that may have some bearing on academic performance. Parents should be made aware of social skills deficits that may contribute to poor social skills.

TYPES OF SOCIAL SKILLS DEFICITS

There are four major types of social skills deficits: (1) skill deficits, (2) inadequate skill performance, (3) performance deficits, and (4) self-control deficits.[1]

1. Skill deficits occur when individuals do not know how to perform the social skill in question.
2. Inadequate skill performance implies that the individual has partly performed the social skill but, due to lack of understanding, has not completed it. An example may be when someone is blamed for an act he or she did not commit. Initially, the person would say that he or she did not commit the act. However, when the other individual keeps insisting, the accused individual may resort to aggressive behavior rather than using negotiation strategies.

3. Performance deficits indicate that the individual knows how to perform a given task but due to physical or other problems does not complete it.
4. Self-control deficits include a variety of behaviors in which the individual cannot control his or her behavior. A multitude of problems may be associated with this deficit. Frequently, individuals have to be taught how to control their behaviors.

EFFECTS OF SOCIAL SKILLS DEFICITS

Social skills training should assume an important place in curricula for African-American males in the home. An increasing number of young African-American males fail to succeed in society because of inadequate social skills. It has been suggested that social skills deficits not only interfere with success in the peer group and educational mainstream but are also predictive of long-term maladaptive behavior patterns, including delinquency, dropping out of school, drug abuse, military discharge for bad conduct, and adult mental health problems, which all may contribute to aggressive and maladjusted behavior. These inappropriate behaviors if not corrected may lead to conflicts with social agencies.

As a result, acquisition of social communication skills is extremely important for these boys, primarily because social communication skills are the foundation of interpersonal competence. Inclusion of social skills training provides the parents with the opportunity to effectively address social skills deficits with collaboration from the school.

Parents should be aware that research has shown that while social skills training packages promote acquisition of socially appropriate behaviors, there is little evidence to suggest that instruction directed at improving students' social competence transfers over time and across cultural settings. Several reasons for this generalization have been presented.

First, social interaction is reciprocal; it involves social exchange among individuals. The limitations and the absence of socially competent peers as models for young African-American males may seriously impair this reciprocity. Training must take place in settings where these students interact with their peers in order for newly acquired skills to be generalized and maintained.

Second, exposure to adequate peer models is insufficient; peers must be trained to provide appropriate models for young black males.[2] Further, social skills training and reinforcement must occur in settings in which these boys interact naturally with their peers.[3]

Third, African-American males must be taught to exhibit behaviors that will be reinforced naturally by peers. Therefore, it is important to select target behaviors that are adaptive and desirable, contribute to the development of social competence, and prompt peer responses that are likely to be reinforcing. The lack of social skills training, inappropriate behavioral activity, and poor interpersonal relationship problems all result in deficits in social skills.

Research has shown a positive relationship between certain social skills and school achievement of African-American males. For example, acts of social communication such as initiating contact about work assignments, asking and answering questions, and engaging in academic-related discussions are experiences needed for appropriate social exchange.[4] Parents tend to place less value on these social communication skills; however, few opportunities for development of social communication are likely to be provided in classrooms for African-American males.

Systematic assessment procedure results are needed to aid the parents in employing appropriate intervention strategies. Assessment results and interventions should be fully explained and demonstrated to parents by school professionals, along with how results and intervention strategies can reduce maladjusted behaviors as well as information and strategies that may prevent early arrest in the teenage years.

ASSESSING SOCIAL SKILLS

Several tests are available for assessing social skills of African-American males. These tests measure all aspects of social behavior and may be classified as formal or informal. Since many of these tests were designed for different populations, they will have to be modified for use with African-American males.

Assessing Social Skills Deficits

Several types of instruments may be used to assess social skills. Commonly used teacher-made tests use several testing formats. These include checklists, observation schedules, rating scales, interviews, direct observations, role play, assessment of social competence, and a variety of inventories covering the gamut of social behaviors.

Anecdotal records may also be used in obtaining data about the boys. These records provide an opportunity to study a student's behavior over a period of time as well as to collect information that is essential in planning instructional programs. Additionally, anecdotal records provide a means of understanding the dynamics of the learner over a period of time.

Taylor[5] stressed the importance of assessing children's social skills during the early years using both formal and informal techniques. Results should be made known to parents as well as interpretations and what the results imply. One of the techniques discussed is the Social Attributes Checklist. Areas covered in this checklist include eight individual skills, fourteen social skills, and two peer relationship attributes. Results from the checklist pinpoint areas of social development in the above attributes that need to be addressed.

The Pediatric Evaluation of Disabilities Inventory is a measure of functional skills in the social function domain. It is also a checklist-type inventory. Haltiwanger[6] used this checklist with a large sample of parents of young children. A major component of the study was to interview these parents to determine the amount of assistance they provided their children for each skill on the checklist. Analysis of the responses showed that children who were successful received at least minimal assistance or supervision from their parents.

Few tests are designed specifically to assess social skills of African-American males. As indicated, most tests have to be modified to assess the social traits of this unique group of males. The reader is referred to a fairly recent issue of Buros's *Mental Measurements Yearbook* for additional tests.[7]

Social skills are difficult to assess due chiefly to issues related to reliability and interpretability. Many social skills are directly associated with one's culture, and when assessed outside of that culture, results can be misleading. Assessment instruments for measuring social skills should be interpreted with the uniqueness of the individual in mind and the type of intervention that is being attempted to change the negative behavior.

APPLICATION OF BEHAVIORAL INTERVENTION STRATEGIES

Learning depends upon the following factors: drive, response, cue, and reward. The principal theoretical concepts drawn from this assumption are reinforcement values and expectations. The tendency for a specific behavior to occur in any given situation is a function of the individual's expectations of reinforcement in that situation and of the value of the reinforcements. Parents will need some assistance from professionals in applying behavioral strategies and research findings. They can employ follow-up strategies at home recommended by the professionals.

The reinforcement values and expectations of some African-American males differ from the values expected at school. Thus, what has been successful for them in their environments may be a source of conflict in the school. In essence, these children have frequently been reinforced by what the school may term "negative behaviors." The goal-driven behaviors, responses to events, and the cues they have developed are frequently a means of survival in their environments. These behaviors work well for them until they attend school. At school, the copying and imitative tendencies learned at home are generally not tolerated or accepted, causing frustration, poor self-image, and sometimes aggressive behavior. [8]

Most boys can learn from rewards and punishments and then proceed to make a judgment in a new social situation as a result of previous experiences. "Social referencing" involves using information from other people to guide behavior and affect ambiguous situations. [9]

Unfortunately, many at-risk African-American males cannot learn effective social skills without direct intervention from parents. Frequently, behavior problems arise in class because successful intervention techniques have not been tried. Most traditional methods do not work for many at-risk African-American males. A learning environment is needed that fosters reduction of negative behaviors and recognizes the uniqueness of the individual.

Hudley [10] used one intervention strategy that appeared to reduce aggressive behavior among males. A sample (101) of aggressive and nonaggressive elementary-school boys was randomly assigned to an attributional intervention and a nontreatment control group. The study was designed to determine the effects of an attribution intervention program on reducing aggressive males' tendency toward ambiguous negative peer interactions. Findings revealed that the experimental group of boys (attributional intervention) showed a significant reduction in hostile intent and disciplinary action as rated by their teachers.

Research by Jewett focused on aggression and cooperation and ways of helping young children use appropriate strategies for coping with them. Jewett asserted that aggression and cooperation share one common element, which emerges from children's strong developmental push to initiate control and maintain relationships with their peers.

Aggression was defined as any intentional act that resulted in physical or mental injury. Aggressive actions can be accidental, instrumental, or hostile acts of behavior. It was noted that aggression should not be confused with assertion. Assertion, in turn, was defined as a process of behavior through which children maintain and defend their rights.

Cooperation, on the other hand, was defined as any activity that involves willing interdependence of two or more students. Cooperation was distinguished from compliance in that compliance denoted obedience to authority rather than intentional cooperation. Aggressive behavior may be reduced by employing strategies that permit students to verbalize their feelings, develop appropriate problem-solving techniques for conflict, and internalize and be cognizant of the effects of their aggressive behaviors upon others.

Collins and Hatch summed up effective strategies for supporting social and emotional growth of young children: (1) model social behavior; (2) establish environments that encourage positive social exchange; (3) encourage children to become aware of the consequences of their behaviors; (4) help children produce acceptable behavior; and (5) encourage the development of children's self-esteem. These behavioral techniques are also designed to make individuals aware of their impact on reacting to and interacting with others.

SUMMARY

One of the valuable roles of teachers is that of being an observer. Observing behavior in the classroom provides valuable information for intervention. Frequently, on the basis of the information supplied, appropriate action can be taken to change negative behaviors. The same rationale may be advanced for other interventions. Equally important is the interpretation of the information from assessment for African-American males. It is recommended here that resource individuals knowledgeable about black cultures be consulted before intervention is attempted.

NOTES

1. T. W. Collins and J. A. Hatch, "Supporting the Social-Emotional Growth of Young Children," *Dimensions of Early Childhood* 21 (1992): 17–21.

2. S. H. Holland, "A Radical Approach to Educating Black Males," *Education Week Commentary* (1987): 24–25.

3. G. R. Taylor, *Three Evaluation Reports on Evaluating Social Skills of Young African-American Males* (reports submitted to Sinclair Lane Elementary School, Baltimore, MD, 1994).

4. A. G. Hilliard, "Teachers and Culture Styles in a Pluralist Society," *NEA Today* 7(6) (1989): 65–69; G. R. Taylor, "Impact of Social Learning Theory on Educating Deprived/Minority Children," Clearinghouse for Teacher Education (Washington, DC: ERIC ED 349260, 1992).

5. G. R. Taylor, *Skills Intervention for Young African-American Males* (Westport, CT: Greenwood, 1997).

6. J. Haltiwanger and Wendy Coster, "A Normative Study of Development in Context: Growth toward Independence in Social Function Skills of Young Children" (paper presented at the biennial meeting of the Society for Research in Child Development, Seattle, WA, April 18–20, 1991), ERIC ED 342504.

7. G. R. Taylor, *Practical Application of Social Learning Theories in Educating Young African-American Males* (Lanham, MD: University Press of America, 2003).

8. Taylor (2003); V. Bronfenbrenner, *The Ecology of Human Development* (Cambridge, MA: Harvard University Press, 1979).

9. F. E. Obiakor, "Self-Concept of African-American Students: An Operational Model for Special Education, *Exceptional Children* 59(2) (1992): 160–67.

10. T. W. Collins and J. A. Hatch, "Supporting the Social-Emotional Growth of Young Children," *Dimensions of Early Childhood* 21 (1992): 17–21.

Chapter Seven

Assessment Strategies

It is incumbent upon educators to be fully apprised of the assessment process. The assessment process collects relevant information on African-American males in order to enable schools to make valid decisions about them in areas of learning and human functioning. It is a multifaceted process, which involves more than the use of a variety of mental, physical, and social tasks. This chapter is designed to address the use of tests to make sound educational decisions. It is also designed to make valid instructional decisions for African-Americans attending schools in urban school districts.[1] Parents' recommendations and suggestions should be reflected in the assessment process. If properly conducted, assessment data will indicate strengths and weaknesses. If weaknesses are not addressed, they may lead to maladaptive behaviors, which may defy the school order.

Cohen and Spenciner[2] articulated that assessment is a global term for observing, fathering, recording, and interpreting information to answer questions and make legal instructional decisions about boys. In essence, assessment is used to make valid decisions about boys in the areas of learning human and social functioning. Assessment is a multifaceted process, which involves more than the use of standardized tests. Informal tests can yield valuable information used in the assessment. The process includes assessing individuals in a variety of mental, physical, and social tasks.[3] Appropriate assessment strategies can enable educators to develop functional and realistic interventions, which may prevent African-American males from committing inappropriate acts that result in criminal behavior. If these inappropriate acts of violence and social norms continue, many African-American males, in particular, may become incarcerated.

DEFINING ASSESSMENT

Sometimes there is confusion regarding the terms *assessment* and *testing.* This confusion should be made clear to parents. While assessment and testing are related, they are not synonymous. Testing is the administration of specifically designed measures of behavior and is part of the assessment process.

Assessment, also known as evaluation, can be seen as a problem-solving process that involves many ways of collecting information about the student. Roth-Smith[4] suggested that this information-gathering process should involve the following formal and informal techniques:

- observing the student's interactions with parents, teachers, and peers;
- interviewing the student and significant others in his or her life;
- examining school records and past evaluation reports;
- evaluating developmental and medical histories;
- using information from checklists completed by parents, teachers, or students themselves;
- evaluating curriculum requirements and options;
- using task analysis to identify which task components have already been mastered and in what order unmastered skills need to be taught; and
- collecting ratings on teachers' attitudes toward African-American males, peer acceptance, and classroom climate.

Clearly, gathering information about the boys using such a variety of techniques and information sources can be expected to shed considerable light upon their strengths and needs, how they affect educational performance, and what type of instructional goals and objectives should be established.

MAJOR TYPES OF ASSESSMENT DEVICES AND STRATEGIES

Several types of assessment devices and strategies are used to make decisions relevant to the abilities and disabilities of African-American males. They are too numerous to be listed in this chapter. The reader should refer to any basic book on assessment when seeking additional information. The purpose of this chapter is to overview the educational use of informal assessment information for evaluating African-American males, including techniques such as observation, portfolio assessment, self-assessment, and various types of tests employed to assess human behavior.[5]

Objective-type tests may be used to supplement or compare results from standardized tests. They may also be employed where standardized tests are not adequate for reasons of content, difficulty, scope, or sensitive cultural materials. Teacher-made tests are based on objectives of the course. A teacher-made test is greatly improved when the teacher knows the principles that govern the writing of objective-type systems and assess them in examinations. These assessment devices are needed to appropriately assess the strengths and weaknesses of African-American males. Caution should be used in the selection of tests. Educators should rule out those instruments that appear to be culturally biased, and they may need to seek professional assistance in these areas. Effective use of assessment data will identify weaknesses in all areas of human functioning in the males and will outline prerequisite skills needed to achieve the standards. Mastering subject content has been proven to decrease the dropout rate, which is highly correlated with incarceration of African-American males.

APPROACH TO ASSESSMENT

Assessment is a complex process that needs to be conducted by a multidisciplinary team of trained professionals and involve both formal and informal methods of collecting information about the males. While the team may choose to administer a series of tests to the student, by law, assessment must involve much more than standardized tests.

To develop a comprehensive view of African-American males, both standardized and nonstandardized tests should be used. In addition, assessment involves evaluating the males' competencies in academics, personality, and socialized physical abilities in order to make valid decisions concerning the instructional program.

MAJOR TYPES OF STANDARD ASSESSMENT TESTS

Assessment tests and instruments have been developed to assess. Once again, parents should be apprised of the selection of tests. They should consider whether or not the tests will promote cognitive and problem-solving skills, academic skills, learning styles, and specific learning needs to successfully deal with solving problems that may cause their child to have conflicts with social agencies. Some tests are paper and pencil, some are tests administered by specialists, some are norm referenced, and others are criterion referenced.

Chiefly, educators use norm- and criterion-referenced tests. These tests are based upon norms of a particular age group. Criterion-referenced tests are based on the curriculum or objectives of a school district.

Norm-Referenced Tests (NRT)

Norm-referenced tests are based upon the average performance of a typical age group using standardized procedures. Items in the tests are designed to provide a sample of curriculum content that students should have had in a certain age group or subject area. An example would be that a fifth-grade student should have been taught multiplication; test items are constructed to measure this skill. Students who score at or above the established score are considered to be on grade level; those who score below the established score are considered to be below grade level. In essence, NRT scores show how students' scores compare with each other within school districts and across the country. NRT scores typically do not fall below the established norm or school. [6]

Types of interpretive scores given on norm tables are grade equivalent, intelligence quotients, mental ages, percentile rank, and stanines. Sometimes raw scores are converted to weighted scores. Standardized or norm-referenced scores are the most objective instruments available for measuring factual recognition, certain skills, concepts, understanding, problem solving, and sometimes personality traits such as interests and attitudes.

Standardized or norm-referenced tests should reflect the following characteristics:

1. They should be available in at least two equivalent forms. It is best to use a different form when pre- and post-testing pupils.
2. They should have acceptable face validity; the tests should look valid.
3. They should use symbols and pictures that are familiar to African-American males.
4. They should reflect descriptive normative data on pupils selected for the normative groups. Educators can match and compare characteristics of the normative group with their pupils before selecting tests.
5. They should have tables reflecting appropriate standard scores in which the raw scores are transposed. Educators may use these tables to convert raw scores to standard scores.

Criterion-Referenced Tests

Unlike norm-referenced tests, criterion-referenced tests may be locally normed. They provide information on how well students are performing based upon the school districts' goals and objectives in various subject areas. They are designed to compare an individual's performance to some criterion or behavior. Test items are constructed to measure the attainment of the stated objectives. Students not performing up to the criterion will probably have difficulty mastering the next instructional sequence. These test items may be constructed in several basic domains from the curriculum. Strategies employed in constructing criterion-referenced tests are beyond the scope of this chapter.

These tests are commonly used to determine how well students have mastered the domains outlined in the curriculum.[7] Several states have begun to employ criterion-referenced testing. These are designed more for individualized instruction than norm-referenced tests. Specific standards have been set for mastery of the curriculum domains. Students not meeting the standard or criterion are judged as working below grade level. Maryland is one state that has adapted criterion-referenced testing statewide. Criterion tests, as with most assessment devices, have some accommodations that will have to be made when assessing children with exceptionalities according to the nature and extent of those exceptionalities.

Many of these tests will have to be modified and adapted for use with African-American males because they may not have the prerequisite skills needed to successfully pass the tests. Additional development work may be initially needed.

ADVANTAGES OF USING STANDARDIZED TESTS

When teachers use multiple assessment factors, they are most likely to determine deficits in learning. In addition, assessment data can assist the teacher in determining the physical and human resources needed to conduct the instructional program.[8] Assessment can also serve as a motivator for African-American males. Educators should encourage these males to improve their performances in weak skill areas by modeling behaviors of successful black professionals and assessing, as well as communicating to the parents and stakeholders how the educators managed to avoid incarceration.

Standardized tests are used to assess the abilities of students in various subject areas and to compare the results to those of a national sample. Results may be used to adapt or modify the instructional program and address the strengths and weaknesses of the students. Many African-American males have not been exposed to much of the information in standardized tests. As a result, many of the items are biased and do not reflect the cultural values of the group. When test results are compared between African-Americans and whites, the disparities are evident.

A national study by the Educational Testing Service and the Education Trust was conducted on eighth-graders.[9] The National Assessment of Education Progress (NAEP) revealed that white students outscored African-American students by twenty-six points (equivalent of more than two years) on the writing assessment and thirty-nine points (or the equivalent of four years) on the mathematics assessment. The informal mode on nonstandardized tests appears to be more suited to the diverse needs of African-American males if they adhere to their cultural differences. Appropriate informal tests may be more suited to assess the strengths and weaknesses. The parents should mandate that educators teach toward the strength of their children, especially African-American males. Motivation and self-concept are increased when the traits are presented, behaviors that cause criminal behaviors are deferred.

CHOOSING APPROPRIATE INFORMAL ASSESSMENT

The type of informal instrument chosen should be appropriate for African-American males and discussed with parents before implementation. These instruments will usually provide information which may reveal areas in need of remediation and if not addressed may lead to conflict with school and social standards. Teachers may use interviews and observations to assist them in choosing and developing appropriate informal assessment instruments. The following strategies and considerations are recommended to assist teachers:

1. Consider the skill areas to be assessed and identify the type of informal testing format to use.
2. Is the content area being assessed appropriate for African-American males?
3. What is the specific purpose of the informal assessment?
4. What accommodations, if any, are needed?
5. Are there available human and physical resources?
6. How similar are the test's contents to actual classroom tasks?

OBSERVATIONS

Observation is a prime assessment strategy. It should be an essential part of assessment. There should be some predetermined system or structure to guide the observational process. Of utmost importance, educators must define the behavior to be observed and select the types of instruments to record the observations.

Educators may use check marks to observe the occurrence of the behaviors or simply write "yes" or "no" to each behavior. These observational data may be used to determine strengths and weaknesses in various areas and indicate areas where intervention will be needed. As indicated, students may be observed in different settings. The teacher should choose those settings and times when the behaviors are most likely to occur. Certain types of behaviors may manifest themselves at certain times in the day. Several types of recording systems may be used, such as event, duration, and interval recording. [10]

ANECDOTAL RECORDS

Anecdotal records provide a written account of the child's behavior. Data from rating scales and checklists may be used to validate narrative statements in anecdotal records concerning African-American males. Educators should exercise caution in recording events and in separating facts from their interpretations of behaviors. Another caution is that of validity; data should be kept over a period of time to note trends.

Educators' biases, known or unknown, tend to influence the information contained in anecdotal records. There is both observer bias and observed bias. Observer bias may be evident from the observer's recording invalid behaviors because of some like or dislike of a special characteristic of the observed. Observed bias may result from the fact that the observed may behave differently simply because they know that they are being observed.

There are many valuable uses of anecdotal records. To be useful in the instructional program, they should be systematically updated and kept over a period of time and used to strengthen the instructional program by programming African-American males' strengths and weaknesses into the curriculum. [11] The teacher must carefully consider the issue of collecting and organizing information in anecdotal records. Some type of systematic plan should be evident. A three-ring binder that is sectioned off alphabetically by students' last names, a separate notebook on each content area, or a card file system may be employed. Anecdotal information can provide a valuable resource for identifying and recognizing trends in specific areas. Programs can be developed to reduce these problem areas, which, if not adequately addressed, can lead to violation of laws.

REVIEWING SCHOOL RECORDS

School records can be a rich source of information about an African-American male's background. The number of times the student has changed schools may be of interest; frequent school changes can be disruptive emotionally as well as academically and may be a factor in the problems that have resulted in the boy's being referred for assessment. Attendance is another area to note; are there patterns in absences (e.g., during a specific part of the year, as is the case with some students who have respiratory problems or allergies), or is there a noticeable pattern of declining attendance, which may be linked to a decline in motivation, an undiagnosed health problem, or a change within the family? We have collaborated on the importance and influence of these factors on the achievement of African-American males.

The student's past history of grades is usually of interest to the assessment team as well. Is the student's current performance in a particular subject typical of the student, or is the problem being observed something new?[12]

Test scores from assessment instruments are also important to review, including data from informal assessments. These assessment data may indicate strengths and weaknesses in several curriculum domains. Based upon the results, a realistic and functional instructional plan can be developed.[13]

Self-assessment can yield valuable information to assist the parents in understanding how their males feel toward educational social involvement issues influencing their perceptions on problems in society. Self-assessment data may come from a variety of sources, such as interviews, journals, log questionnaires, checklists, and rating scales. The construction of the instruments used in self-assessment must consider the development level of African-American males in all of the principal areas such as mental, social, and physical. In the case of the boys, the type of cultural experience must be carefully considered. In some instances, the teacher will have to assist the child in completing his or her self-assessment.[14] The experiences deviate considerably in the lifestyles of the boys, and the information presented can be infused into the instructional program. This approach will make learning functional and realistic by relating real experiences to the curriculum.

The values of using portfolios in assessing the strengths and weaknesses of African-American males have been well documented in the professional literature.[15] Effective portfolio assessment requires a cooperative effort on the part of the teachers, children, and sometimes parents. The assessment should reflect the learning as well as the products of learning. The teachers should develop scoring rubrics with input from the boys. They should be instructed on how to use the scoring rubrics. The teachers, boys, and parents should review objective information periodically to update, delete, document, or expand information items selected for inclusion. Items should be directly related to objectives specified in the instructional program. Several authors cited have advocated that captions should be developed to: (1) identify the document, (2) show a description of the content, (3) explain why items were included, and (4) summarize and synthesize information.

TYPES OF RECORDINGS

Several types of recordings are necessary to record information from assessment instruments and devices. Data from these recordings may indicate to parents the need for intervention to change inappropriate behaviors. Event recording involves recording specific behavior. Interval recording is reserved for specific times to record behaviors. Teachers should select the types of recording they deem best for recording the behaviors of the boys. In general, short observations conducted over a period of time are frequently the best methods to employ to record test results for African-American males.

TEACHER-MADE AND INFORMAL TESTS

Teacher-made and informal tests may be used to supplement or compare results from standardized tests to develop functional activities with consultation and modify maladaptive behaviors that may lead to conflicts with the law. They may also be employed where standardized tests are not adequate for reasons of content, difficulty, scope, or sensitive cultural materials to African-American males. Teacher-made tests are based on objectives of the course. One of the first things a teacher should consider when constructing a test is the type of test format to be employed. There are several types of testing formats: (1) true-false, (2) multiple choice, (3) matching, (4) completion, and (5) essay. The type of format chosen will greatly depend upon the types of learning experiences of the boys. Several adaptations and modifications may need to be made in the testing command and response.

A variety of teacher-made and informal assessment devices and techniques such as observations, questionnaires, interviews, and inventories are at the disposal of the classroom teacher. Informal assessments provide information relevant to the boys' current level of performance and assist in pinpointing goals, objectives, and needed adaptation and modification in the instructional program. Performance should be compared with specific learning tests or objectives within the curricula. These techniques permit the direct assessment of student behavior that may be compared with norm-referenced test data and may be adapted for use with African-American males.

QUESTIONNAIRES

Questionnaires may be developed to fit different formats such as surveys, checklists, rating scales, and multiple-choice, matching, completion, and true-false items. Questionnaires are designed to collect specific information from students. Little training is needed in constructing questionnaires. The only requirement is knowledge of the content being solicited. Questionnaires are easily administered and scored.

INTERVIEWS

For many African-American males, rather than using questionnaires, alternate means must be evident for collecting information. The boys' lack of academic training and experiences frequently prohibit them from responding to questionnaires appropriately. Interviews may be substituted to elicit information. The teacher may control the length and time and provide direction during the interviewing process. Frequently, teachers need detailed information that interviews can provide. Parents and other professionals must be interviewed to secure the necessary information. The validity of information secured from interviews greatly depends upon the accuracy of the information provided by the interviewer. Teachers must be aware and proceed with caution when interpreting information.

INVENTORIES AND SUBJECT MATTER TESTS

Inventories and subject matter tests may be used to assess a variety of skills in curricula areas for African-American males that may be employed to offset behaviors that may result in criminal behavior. Parents should be notified of the results and strategies for assisting African-American males in changing inappropriate behaviors. They provide information on the males' present levels of functioning with the curriculum. Inventories may be developed by the teacher or purchased commercially for many subject areas. In designing inventories and subject matter tests, teachers should be knowledgeable about

1. assessing the curriculum area being tested;
2. developmentally appropriate skills;
3. breaking tasks or skills into small manageable parts;
4. preparing test items for each subtest of the curriculum being assessed;
5. adapting and modifying the number of test items based upon the cultural backgrounds of the boys;
6. sequencing the test items from easiest to the most difficult degree.

ALTERNATIVE ASSESSMENT

Elliott and Gresham[16] stated that alternative assessment is a substitute way of gathering meaningful information on students' learning for those who are unable to take, even with accommodations, the regular assessment. Many African-American males in the cognitive, social, and physical domains are enrolled in different courses of studies because their lack of education preparation does not permit them to complete the regular curriculum successfully. Typically, these boys are working on social skills curricula. These experiences are designed to develop interpersonal skills, which are necessary for academic success and adhering to social norms. Parental suggestions should be initiated concerning the type of alternative assessment to be used.

Alternative assessment may involve using several formats. Portfolio assessment is commonly used in conducting alternative assessment. As indicated earlier, portfolio assessments may include summaries and examples of all of the student's learning, which is checked by the teacher and updated frequently. Other informal types of assessment instruments are rating scales, checklists, questionnaires, surveys, interviews, and self-report inventories.[17]

PLANNING OBJECTIVE-TYPE TESTS

The first step in planning a teacher-made test is to write specifications for the test. The culture values of the African-American male should constitute the nature of the specification being used. Essay types may not be the best type to use based upon assessment strategies employed, and parental involvement is highly encouraged. The purpose must be clearly articulated. Steps include arranging items in order of difficulty, preparing directions for administering the test, setting time limits, conducting an item analysis, constructing a scoring system, and establishing reliability and validity for the test. Specifications need to be written for each subject area tested. Subject areas will determine the nature and extent of the specification written. Teachers may need some assistance in completing the aforementioned steps, especially in conducting an item analysis and establishing reliability and validity. It is recommended that teachers consult with a psychology research and evaluation department at a local university or with the school system research and evaluation department.

One of the first things a teacher should consider in constructing a test is the type of test format to be employed, as well as the objectives of the course. There are several types of testing formats: (1) true-false, (2) multiple choice, (3) matching, (4) completion, (5) essay (6) questionnaires, (7) interviews, and (8) inventories and subject matter tests. [18] The type of format chosen will greatly depend upon prior learning experiences and the type of curriculum innovations to which the African-American male has been exposed. For example, an essay type may not be suited to a child who has not developed good writing skills. Several adaptations and modifications may need to be made in the testing command and response.

The aforementioned testing formats can be scored in various ways. In some instances, the raw scores of correct responses can simply be counted up and a letter grade assigned. In other cases, points can be assigned and converted to letter grades. One of the newest ways to score teacher-made objective tests is through the application of rubrics.

A second step for teachers is to decide on the type of objective test items to be used. This is explained in greater detail later in this chapter. In choosing a testing format, teachers should determine the following factors:

- a description of the test;
- the purpose for giving the test;
- the nature and extent of students' disabilities;
- the number of items to be presented;
- timing of the test;
- a preterm analysis of the test items, eliminating those items that are too easy or difficult, and rewriting items based upon the analysis.

A third step is to arrange the items in order of difficulty from easy to hard. For many African-American males, a series of easy items may be infused with hard ones to develop confidence and self-esteem.

A fourth step is to prepare directions for administering the test. Directions should come at the beginning of each part. The time limit should be set based upon the ages and other abilities and disabilities of the children. For some

African-American males, accommodations may need to be made, such as increasing the time for them to complete the items or reading the items to them and recording their responses.

A fifth step is that teachers should be skilled in using and communicating assessment results when making decisions about individual students' instructional programs relevant to school and society.

A sixth step is for teachers to skillfully develop valid student grading procedures that use results from student assessments. Teachers using this standard will have justification for their grading system, which will be based upon assessment data.[19]

A seventh step is to recognize unethical, illegal, and otherwise inappropriate assessment methods and use of assessment information. In order to use the standard effectively, teachers will have to be knowledgeable about local and state laws governing ethical standards relating to testing and assessment. Major testing formats are described below.[20]

Other Factors to Be Considered

Writing Specifications for the Test

The purpose of the test must be clearly articulated and specifications for the test developed. Steps include arranging items in order of difficulty, preparing directions for administering the test, setting the time limit, conducting an item analysis, constructing a scoring system, and establishing reliability and validity of the test based upon cultural norms.

Use of Informal Assessment Data

If informal assessment data are to be effectively used to gauge to what extent the stated objectives have been achieved, they must be administered to students before and after instruction begins, to assist in

1. evaluating the competence in a particular skill;
2. determining the baseline behavior for a particular skill;
3. using results to revise the unit;
4. providing information to gauge the progress of African-American males;
5. appraising the effectiveness of selected skill activities;
6. making sure that the students have the necessary prerequisites for performing the skills;
7. having the necessary physical and human instruction;
8. eliciting the cooperation of parents;
9. providing training for parents to follow up at home;

10. determining the reactions of students; and
11. determining what accommodations will be needed, to overcome deficits imposed by the environment.

Specific techniques for evaluating the skills development of African-American males are many. There are several informal techniques that may be used to determine the degree of social deficits. Not addressing these deficits may be related to the percentage of African-American males committing criminal acts.

1. Develop a brief checklist to assess skills in a variety of situations.
2. Stimulate social, academic, and psychomotor activities requiring the students to portray different roles that can be used to assess the understanding of appropriate behaviors in various settings. The class may conduct group and individual appraisal of the activity.
3. Use group assignments to evaluate the ability of the students to work cooperatively. Record specific incidents, both appropriate and inappropriate.
4. Model and provide illustrations of appropriate and inappropriate behaviors.
5. Structure activities and situations that call for specific kinds of behaviors and observe the performance of the students. A rating scale may be used.
6. Assess the frequency of inappropriate behaviors and assist the students in monitoring their own behaviors.
7. Use a variety of audiovisual aids, such as films and filmstrips, depicting appropriate and inappropriate social skills, and have the students critique.
8. Use learning styles to assess how the students input and output information. What is taking place? Give alternative responses.

EVALUATING LEARNING STYLES

Pupils learn through a variety of sensory channels and demonstrate individual patterns of sensory strengths and weaknesses.[21] Parents should capitalize on African-American male sudents learning styles. Several aspects are recommended when considering factors that characterize a pupil's learning style:

1. The speed at which a student is learning is an important aspect to consider. The learning rate is not as obvious as it may appear. Frequently, a learner's characteristics interfere with his natural learning rate. Although the learning rate is more observable than other characteristics, it does not necessarily relate to the quality of the learner's performance. Therefore, it is of prime importance for the parent to know as much as possible about all of a learner's characteristics.

2. The techniques the students use to organize materials they plan to learn also needs to be considered. Individuals organize materials they expect to learn information from by remembering the broad ideas. These broad ideas trigger the details in the student's memory. This method of proceeding from the general to the specific is referred to as a deductive style of organization. This principle may be applied successfully in many situations. Other pupils prefer to remember the smaller components, which then reminds them of the broader concept, using an inductive style of organizational thought. In utilizing inductive organization, the pupil may look at several items or objectives and form specific characteristics, then develop general principles or concepts. Knowing a student's style of organizational thought can assist the parent in effectively guiding the learning process by presenting materials as closely as possible to the student's preferred style or organization.

3. The learner's need for reinforcement and structure in the learning situation is also important. All learners need some structure and reinforcement to their learning. This process may be facilitated through a student's preferred channels of input and output.

4. Input involves using the five sensory channels—auditory, visual, tactile and kinesthetic, olfactory, and gustatory—which are transmitted to the brain. In the brain, the sensory stimuli are organized into cognitive patterns referred to as the input channel through which the person readily processes stimuli using his preferred mode or modality.

5. Similar differences are evident in output, which may be expressed verbally or nonverbally. Verbal output uses the fine-motor activity of the speech mechanism to express oral language. Nonverbal output uses both fine- and gross-motor activities. Fine-motor skills may include gesture and demonstration. Learners usually prefer to express themselves through one of these channels.

6. A student's preferred mode of input is not necessarily his or her strongest acuity channel. Sometimes a student transfers information received through one channel into another with which he or she is more comfortable. This process is called intermodal transfer. Learners differ in their ability to perform the intermodal transfer. Failure to perform this task effectively may impede learning.

The differences in learning styles and patterns of some pupils almost ensure rewarding educational achievement for successful completion of tasks. Unfortunately, this is not true for many young African-American males. The differences reflected in learning can interfere with the student's achievement. Early identification, assessment, and management of a student's learning differences can prevent more serious learning problems from occurring.

Some children are concrete learners while others are abstract learners. Some focus on global aspects of a problem, others on specific points. Ideally, a student should be flexible enough to do both. Since schools traditionally give more weight to analytical than to holistic approaches, the student who does not manifest analytical habits is at a decided disadvantage. [22]

Parents presenting information to their children through their strongest modality accomplish a two-way objective. First, information is readily received and understood; second, understanding of concepts improves achievement. High achievement tends to reduce negative behavior and promote positive behavior. Basic academic and social concepts can facilitate and enable the learner to understand and demonstrate these basic concepts.

Parents who use the concept of learning styles can facilitate the learning of their child by presenting information through their strongest modality. This approach encourages the males to process and understand information that they normally would not understand if that information were presented through their weakest modality. When concepts and information are presented to the male learners in ways such that they can comprehend the academic and social tasks, inappropriate behaviors are eliminated or reduced. Parents who teach their African-American male children to internalize their behaviors before they act them out are not likely to permit socially rejected behaviors that may lead to criminal behavior and arrest.

Additionally, experiences and activities should be sequenced so that stated goals and objectives may be effectively achieved. [23]

Figure 7.1 displays how an effective assessment model can be constructed with parental input and implemented to judge the skill levels of African-American males and thus reduce the impact of behaviors that may result in incarceration.

The proposed model is uniquely different from the traditional model. The traditional model places emphasis first on the curriculum, followed by instruction and evaluation. The major disadvantage in using the traditional model is that there is no objective way that educators can determine how well objectives have been achieved because no attempt is made to determine students' prior skills in the subjects. On the other hand, the proposed model maintains that the success of any instructional program cannot be fully realized until some initial assessment is made before engaging African-American males in the instructional process. It is practically impossible to determine to

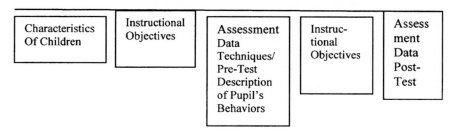

Figure 7.1. Assessment Model

what degree objectives have been achieved unless some precriterion and postcriterion tests have been administered. Pretesting is deemed important for several reasons; it is used to

1. determine whether stated objectives are realistic and functional;
2. guide educators in redefining objectives;
3. provide description of the boys' behavior in curriculum areas;
4. plan for individual differences based upon the objectives and an assessed description of the boys' behaviors; and
5. effectively plan the instructional program based upon the assessed data.

If the assessed data produces negative results, then the results should be corrected before instruction moves to the next step.

Long- and short-term evaluation requires a definite statement of objectives. Evaluation concerns the extent to which goals have been attained and can only pose sensible questions when the long- and short-term goals are clearly stated.[24] To be effective, evaluation must be a continuous process and must provide an answer to two basic questions: (1) is there evidence of students' growth, and (2) are the experiences received worthwhile for the students?

Various forms of assessment techniques, such as objective tests, checklists, questionnaires, rating scales, and interest inventories may be administered on a pre- or postassessment basis to determine whether the objectives have been achieved and to refine the instructional program if evaluation data indicate that this is necessary.[25]

The proposed model will assist in assuring that instructional planning will be more functional and based upon the assessed needs of African-American males because of pre- and postassessment strategies implemented. Teachers will be better able to judge the level of skill development of the African-American males when the instruction has ended.

SUMMARY

Assessment data are designed to be used as diagnostic tools to determine strengths and weaknesses of African-American males, as well as providing information to improve positive behaviors, which will lessen the probability of African-American males being incarcerated in later years. Data from assessment should be used to direct and guide the instructional program, the learning process, and the instructional design dictating the types of assessment to be used. Both standardized (formal) and teacher-made (nonstandardized) tests may be used to assess African-American males.

Most school districts mandate the use of standardized tests to judge and compare students' learning on the local, state, and national levels. Results may be valuable in providing information relevant to how well expected standards and outcomes have been achieved. Many federally funded programs require that school districts report the progress of students by standardized test scores. Generally, African-American males do not score as well on standardized tests. There are many factors attributed to this dilemma, such as situational, socioeconomic and cultural bias related to test items. For example, test items may not be culture free. Generally, African-American males are not included in the normative samples; thus, their skills and experiences are not included in the tests.[26]

As indicated, nonstandardized tests may be used to give a more realistic and functional assessment of African-American males abilities because they should be based upon the instructional program. Biases in test items are significantly reduced because test items should reflect the focal experiences of the students. Parents should be provided with the results of assessment and trained to facilitate the use of the results in instructing African-American males in social and interpersonal skills.

NOTES

1. G. R. Taylor, *Curriculum Strategies: Social Skills Intervention for Young African-American Males* (Westport, CT: Greenwood, 1997); J. Salvia and J. E. Ysseldyke, *Assessment* (Boston: Houghton-Mifflin, 1998); J. C. Witt, S. N. Elliott, E. J. Daly III, F. M. Gresham, and J. Kramer, *Assessment of At-Risk and Special Needs Children* (New York: McGraw-Hill, 1988).

2. G. L. Cohen and J. L. Spenciner, *Assessment of Children and Youth* (New York: Addison Wesley Longman, 1998).

3. G. R. Taylor, *Using Human Learning Strategies in the Classroom* (Lanham, MD: Scarecrow Press, 2002).

4. C. Roth-Smith, *Learning Disabilities: The Interaction of Learner, Task and Setting* (Boston: Allyn & Bacon, 1991).

5. J. McLoughlin and R. Lewis, *Assessing Special Students: Strategies and Procedures*, 3rd ed. (Columbus, OH: Merrill, 1991); D. M. Browder, *Assessment of Individuals with Severe Disabilities: An Applied Behavior Approach to Life Skills Assessment*, 2nd ed. (Baltimore, MD: Brookes, 1991).

6. Salvia and Ysseldyke (1998); M. H. Epstein, W. D. Bursuck, E. A. Pollowa, C. Cumbland, and M. Jyanthi, "Homework, Grading and Testing: National Surveys of School District Policies," *OSER's News* 5(4) (1993): 15–21.

7. Witt et al. (1988).

8. D. A. Kolb, *Experimental Learning: Experience as a Source of Learning and Development* (Englewood Cliffs, NJ: Prentice-Hall, 1984).

9. Educational Testing Service and the Education Trust, *National Assessment of Educational Progress* (Princeton, NJ: Educational Testing Service and the Education Trust, 1998).

10. K. Pike and S. Salend, "An Authentic Assessment Strategy," *Teaching Exceptional Children* 28(1) (1995): 15–19.

11. L. Rhodes and S. Nathenson-Mejia, "Anecdotal Records: A Powerful Tool for Ongoing Literacy Assessments," *Reading Teacher* 45(7) (1992): 502–9.

12. B. B. Waterman, *Assessing Children in the Presence of a Disability* (Washington, DC: National Information Center for Children and Youth with Disabilities, 1994).

13. C. Hoy and N. Gregg, *Assessment: The Special Educator's Role* (Pacific Grove, CA: Brooks/Cole, 1984); G. R. Taylor, *Educational Interventions and Services for Children with Exceptional Qualities* (Springfield, IL: Charles C. Thomas, 2001).

14. D. M. Davison and D. L. Pearce, "The Influence of Writing Activities on the Mathematics Learning of Native American Students," *Journal of Educational Issues of Language Minority Students* 10 (1992): 147–57.

15. T. Salinger, "Getting Started with Alternative Assessment Methods" (workshop presented at the New York State Reading Association Conference, Lake Kiamesha, New York, 1992); J. M. Wolf, "Just Read," *Education Leadership* 55(8) (1998): 61–63; Taylor (1997).

16. S. N. Elliott and F. M. Gresham, "Social Skills Interventions for Children," *Behavior Modification* 17 (1993): 287–313.

17. Witt et al. (1988).

18. P. W. Airasian, *Classroom Assessment: Concepts and Application*, 4th ed. (New York: McGraw-Hill, 2001).

19. R. L. Marzano, *Transforming Classroom Grading* (Alexandria, VA: Association for Supervision and Curriculum Development, 2001).

20. Airasian (2001).

21. G. R. Taylor, *Practical Application of Social Learning Theories in Educating Young African-American Males* (Lanham, MD: University Press of America, 2003).

22. A. G. Hilliard, "Teachers and Culture Styles in a Pluralist Society," *NEA Today* 7(6) (1989): 65–69.

23. J. Choate, B. Enright, P. Miller, J. Poteet, and R. Rakes, *Curriculum-Based Assessment and Programming*, 3rd ed. (Boston: Allyn & Bacon, 1995).

24. Taylor (2001).

25. G. R. Taylor, *Curriculum Models and Strategies for Education Individuals with Disabilities in Inclusive Classrooms* (Springfield, IL: Charles C. Thomas, 1999); G. R. Taylor, *Parental Involvement: A Practical Guide for Collaboration and Teamwork for Students with Disabilities* (Springfield, IL: Charles C. Thomas, 2000).

26. R. Zurcher, "Issues and Trends in Culture: Fair Assessment," *Intervention in School and Clinic* 34 (1998): 1–6; A. L. Nitko, *Educational Tests and Measurement: An Introduction* (New York: Harcourt Brace, 1983); L. G. Weiss, A. Prifitera, and G. Roid, "The WISE III and the Fairness of Predicting Achievement across Ethnic and Gender Groups," *Journal of Psychoeducational Assessment,* Monograph Series: Advances in Psychoeducational Assessment (1993): 35–42.

Chapter Eight

A Proposed Model for Closing the Achievement Gap

Educational achievements of African-American males have shown a steady decline in this country. Most of the decline has taken place in urban communities where an influx of African-American males reside. There are multiple reasons why these individuals are not achieving up to expected standards. Reasons for this lack of achievement can be attributed to the following that schools must face on a regular and daily basis: (1) political, (2) economic, (3) social, (4) technological, and (5) teacher preparation.[1]

POLITICAL

Politically, many diverse communities are deeply divided on policies involving the administration and structure of public schools. Legislatures associated with school improvement can unite the various diverse groups in the community by exerting control on funding and resources to support the schools and agencies associated with them and through collaboration between and among agencies serving the schools. Public officials' interventions are needed in setting up early intervention programs. This can offset some of the deprivations contributing to the achievement gap.[2] Political issues may incorporate principles from all of the learning theories in assessing and developing political views that govern the schools.

ECONOMIC

There have been major shifts in economic activity in the country during the late twentieth and early twenty-first centuries from industrial-type employment to service-type activities. As a result, many of the service-type jobs were relocated into the suburbs due chiefly to the social and economic conditions in the cities. This resulted in massive exits from the central cities. This loss of a viable tax base was chiefly related to decay in public schools within the cities and perpetuated the increase in the achievement gap. [3]

Schools serving African-American males have traditionally been underfunded. The tax base has been significantly reduced due to the rate of exodus of taxpayers from the central cities. Median family income also decreased as middle-income taxpayers left the central cities. This exodus left central cities with insufficient funds to operate the schools. Local, state, and federal agencies must contribute additional funds to make the schools safe, provide additional resources, advance technology, and employ competent staff. It is the democratic right of all learners, including minorities, to be educated in safe schools with adequate funding and competent personnel. Economic conditions must be improved in central cities if the achievement gap is to be decreased. Integration of the three learning theories identified in previous chapters will have relevance for addressing the economic issues confronted by the schools.

SOCIAL

Cultural and social values of African-American male learners may differ significantly from learners in the mainstream because of a lack of cultural identity. Children's socioeconomic status should have no effect on how teachers judge their abilities to learn. Teachers who classify children into social class membership tend to show their prejudice toward selected groups of children. One major condition for enhancing self-esteem in the classroom is the teacher's acceptance of the child. By accepting the child, the teacher indicates to the child that he or she is worthy of the teacher's attention and respect.

Another condition that promotes self-esteem is the presence of explicit limits in the classroom that are articulated early and are consistently enforced. Such limits should involve input from the children. They should participate in defining acceptable behavior, provide standards of conduct, and establish behavior expectations in the classroom and school. Standards and regulations are necessary for children to develop positive self-esteem because they set limits and expectations. [4]

Educators can abstract from theories of conditioning and social learning a number of ways to improve negative behavior and promote positive behavior. Using rewards, reinforcement, modeling limitation, and observation are major principles in these theories. Techniques in these theories can be readily adaptive or modified to change behaviors in the classroom. Demonstration of appropriate behaviors can aid in closing the achievement gap by reducing inappropriate behavior. Refer to previous chapters for specific strategies to improve the social and cultural values taught in schools.

MEETING STANDARDS

Standards for achievement are reflected in the core curriculum. Many African-American males and deprived learners cannot meet the expected standards due to test items that are not correlated with the curriculum, test items that do not reflect the cultural values of the learners, not enough instructional time for learners to master the content, insufficient time spent teaching critical thinking skills, and the overall poor quality of instruction. In order to determine learners' strengths and weaknesses, valid and reliable assessment information is needed. Assessment should drive the instructional program. To achieve this end, it must be valid and reliable.

Assessment is a key component in educational reforms. Achievement and the progress of children are judged based on set of local, state, or professional standards. A student's performance is measured in relationship to how well the student meets standards. It was assumed that assessment provided sufficient data on how well students were performing in school. More recent data suggest that assessment has not provided sufficient information on what students know and are capable of doing relative to standards. To accurately determine strengths and weaknesses of students, multiple assessments other than standardized tests should be used, such as teacher-made tests, criterion-referenced tests, and other informal tests to determine the achievement gap. [5] Principles from all of the learning theories discussed in the previous chapters are recommended in order to develop effective assessment tools to evaluate the progress of children.

TEACHER PREPARATION

Teacher preparation is an important factor in closing the achievement gap. Teachers must be specifically trained to teach African-American males and deprived learners to achieve stated standards. Teacher training programs housed in institutes of higher learning and in-service programs must alter their approaches in educating teachers about instructing African-American males and deprived learners.[6]

Recommended strategies based on the above research include the following:

1. Teachers must be trained to assume responsibility for students' achievement. The first step is to set high expectations for all students.
2. Demonstrate to students that their contributions are valued and that they can achieve.
3. Consider diversity, languages, and cultures as strengths and infuse them within the instructional program.
4. Relate school experiences to students' homes and communities.
5. Become aware of one's own cultural biases and develop techniques for objectively correcting them.
6. Provide information on how knowledge of learning styles can be employed in the classroom to minimize the achievement gap.
7. Demonstrate and model teaching strategies such as reciprocal teaching, conceptual learning, critical thinking, and problem solving.
8. Provide additional emphasis on community and parental involvement and classroom management techniques.
9. Implement an objective system of interviewing for admitting only those prospective learners who show a commitment for raising the academic level of all learners.
10. Provide prospective teacher observations and field experiences in diverse communities.
11. Establish consortiums for prospective teachers in multicultural education as part of the degree requirements.
12. Provide assistance for teachers to become highly effective and certified.
13. Provide opportunities for student teachers to observe excellent teaching skill sets during their practicum and student-teaching experiences.

All of the learning theories summarized in the previous chapters can be incorporated in preparing teachers to instruct African-American males in the content areas to develop knowledge bases needed to increase achievement.

COLLABORATION

Taylor[7] remarked that schools cannot effectively educate students without collaborating with parents and the community on a continuous basis. Effective collaborative strategies may include problem-solving groups, discussion groups, and conferences. Participation and collaboration are impeded if educators do not view parents and community as competent. Research findings have shown that parental and community attitudes are difficult to accept by the school. Educators must find creative ways to assist some parents in changing their negative ways.[8] A collaborative effort must be made by local, state, and federal agencies to assist school systems in decreasing the achievement gap. Schools alone are not able to bring significant improvement in closing the achievement gap unless there is strong professional and community support with interagency collaboration.

LOCAL INTERVENTION

Collaboration and participation at local school districts may be improved if teachers (1) accept and incorporate parents' knowledge of their children's abilities, both their strengths and weaknesses; (2) provide a structure for parents and communities to express themselves; (3) provide opportunities for parents' participation with their children; (4) teach parents about their rights as parents of school children; (5) develop strategies for making parents welcome in the school; and (6) show empathy, not sympathy, to parents. These are a few strategies teachers can use.

STATE INTERVENTION

State intervention is designed to set standards for collaboration in local school districts, to report on progress of schools in the state, and to provide assistance to schools that are not achieving standards. The state also develops and monitors policies, enforces federal regulations associated with collaboration, and regulates assessment strategies in local school districts. School buildings and construction are maintained by the state, as well as through financial support to the districts.

FEDERAL INTERVENTION

The federal government has contributed billions of dollars to school systems to pay for individual services in the basic skills areas. These funds have had some impact on closing the gap; however, the impact has not significantly reduced the gap in student learning.[9] Collaboration on all fronts is needed to decrease the achievement gap. Each learning theory has specific principles to improve collaboration.

A MODEL FOR CLOSING THE ACHIEVEMENT GAP

The achievement gap in school districts serving a large number of African-American males is increasing. Factors and conditions responsible for this gap have been identified throughout the text. Data presented have shown that the achievement gap can be closed if school districts adhere to the following strategies:

1. Employ certified and highly effective teachers.
2. Provide venues to help raise the tolerance levels of teachers.
3. Have teachers set realistic expectations for students.
4. Increase parental and community involvement.
5. Equip the schools with state-of-the-art technology.
6. Choose unbiased tests to measure achievement.
7. Hold students to articulated standards.
8. Use learning principles from each learning theory.[10]

The listed strategies cannot be successful in closing the achievement gap unless some objective system is developed for school systems to use. The proposed system involves using principles for learning theories to close the gap. The learning theories believed to be associated with classroom learning have been summarized in previous chapters.

CONDITIONING THEORIES

In summary, principles under conditioning theory may aid in closing the achievement gap by rewarding and reinforcing learners for high achievement and performance, evaluating and shaping behaviors, conditioning learners, motivating drill and practice, and reducing negative behavior. These theories indicate that processes governing behaviors are learned. Both the drives that initiate behavior and the specific behavior motivated by these drivers are learned through interactions with the environment. Conditioning and behaviorism have made significant impact upon learning and computer technology. When students are rewarded for learning, their achievement and learning outcomes increase.

SOCIAL LEARNING THEORIES

The role of social learning theories may assist in closing the achievement gap by having students practice and demonstrate good modeling, observing and initiating appropriate social behavior, and developing self-efficacy, social skills, and self-regulation. Social learning theories offer the school a common context through which environment, developmental sequence, and early experiences of individuals' development can be understood. These theories enable educators to better understand how individuals think, how they feel about themselves, and how they become more aware of factors in their environment that may have some bearing on academic performance. There is a significant relationship between social skills interventions and academic achievement. Many social skills procedures, such as attending and positive interaction techniques, have been shown to increase academic performance.

COGNITIVE THEORIES

Cognitive learning has led to improving our understanding of the social nature of learning, the importance of context on understanding, the need for domain-specific knowledge in higher-order thinking, expert-novice differences in thinking and problem solving, and the belief that learners can be instructed to construct their own understanding of a topic. Variables such as drive, habits, and strengths have critical roles in learning. Learning is developmental, and children must master each task before mastering advanced tasks. Learning is facilitated by the child's acquisition of new skills and experiences. How children interpret and receive information can accelerate or impede learning. Identifying and assessing learning styles are important in evaluating achievement.

SUMMARY

Yancey and Saporito[11] articulated that the combined effects of concentrated poverty, cultural diversity, and isolation of deprived neighborhoods by race, ethnicity, and socioeconomic status combine to widen the achievement gap. Educators must explore individualized approaches to educate learners. Using one teaching approach for all learners has proved ineffective. Achievement of all learners can be increased. If cultural values are infused within the curriculum and expectations for learners are raised, learning will increase and students can achieve at expected levels. Research findings have clearly shown that the achievement gap can be successfully closed if innovative and functional practices are used to assist African-American male learners to overcome the negative effects of their environments. The use of learning theories holds the promise of closing the achievement gap.[12] Many of the negative overtones can be reduced by involving learners in activities that appeal to their interests and real-life encounters while assisting them in recognizing the association of parts in formulating wholes.

NOTES

1. G. R. Taylor, *Classroom Management Theories into Practice* (Lanham, MD: University Press of America, 2004).

2. Taylor (2004).

3. G. R. Taylor, *Practical Application of Social Learning Theories in Educating Young African-American Males* (Lanham, MD: University Press of America, 2003).

4. Taylor (2004).

5. G. R. Taylor, T. Phillips, and D. Joseph, *Assessment Strategies for Students with Disabilities* (Lewiston, NY: Edwin Mellen Press, 2002).

6. G. R. Taylor, *Curriculum Strategies: Social Skills Intervention for Young African-American Males* (Westport, CT: Greenwood, 1997); Taylor (2003); E. Garcia, "Language, Culture, and Education," *Review of Research Education* 19 (1993); C. Monteceinois, "Multicultural Teacher Education for a Culturally Diverse Teaching Force," in *Practicing What We Preach: Confronting Diversity in Teacher Education*, R. Marth, ed. (Albany: SUNY Press, 1995); B. Weiner, *Theories of Motivation: From Mechanisms to Cognition* (Chicago: Markham, 1972); K. Zeichner and S. Melnick, "The Role of Community Field Experiences in Preparing Teachers for Cultural Diversity" (paper presented at the annual meeting of the American Association of Colleges of Teacher Education, Chicago, IL, 1995).

7. Taylor (2004).

8. L. Bank, J. H. Marlowe, J. B. Reid, G. R. Patterson, and M. R. Weinrott, "A Comparative Evaluation of Parent-Training Intervention for Families of Chronic Delinquents," *Journal of Abnormal Child Psychology* 19 (1991): 15–33.

9. Commission on Chapter I, *Making Schools Work for Children in Poverty* (Washington, DC: American Association for Higher Education, 1992).

10. Taylor (2004).

11. Taylor (2004).

12. Taylor (2004).

Chapter Nine

Coordination and Utilization of the Community Resources

The reform initiatives outlined in this chapter will depend on the individual needs and resources of communities and school districts. School districts and communities should adapt and modify instruction based upon current research in the field.[1] These trends outline ways and strategies to reduce incarceration of African-American males.

A well-developed research design should be implemented to determine how effective these strategies have been in reducing incarceration. School districts and parents must depend heavily upon valid and reliable data sources to measure progress. In some instances, parents may need to seek consultants outside of the school system.[2]

Parents should insist upon a well-defined plan that specifies incremental steps and assigned priorities. Fullan's[3] view is that

> Most change theorists and practitioners agree that significant changes should be attempted, and alo carried out in a more incremental development way. Large plans and vague ideas make a lethal combination. Significant change can be accomplished by taking a developmental approach, building in more and more components of the change over time. One or two steps at a time.

Reynolds, Teddlie, Hopkins, and Stringfield[4] gave an excellent example of using incremental steps in planning reforms. Using a school where reforms were being made, they observed that "the school did not attempt to implement the whole curriculum and instructional program all at once, but gradually, grade by grade level. In this way, it was possible to prepare teachers for the next grade level using a cascade model."

MODEL DEVELOPMENT

The model articulated in this chapter is premised upon reform research cited in this text. The model is designed to show how the various subsystems can be integrated and infused to provide equality of educational opportunities for African-American males. The model outlines how standards, training, qualification, and performance of school personnel are needed to deter African-American males from being incarcerated. The model is designed to work in conjunction with local and state accountability models and is based upon a study conducted by Marzano.[5]

Marzano[6] developed a comprehensive questionnaire for assessing needs and inducing educational reforms. This comprehensive questionnaire posed specific questions in the areas of (1) curriculum, (2) goals and feedback, (3) parent and community involvement, (4) safe and orderly environment, (5) collegiality and professionalism, (6) home environment, (7) budget and finance, (8) closing the achievement gap, (9) student motivation, (10) instruction, (11) classroom management, and (12) classroom curriculum design.

Details concerning these factors are reflected through Marzano's[7] text and constitute the components of the model. Specific questions are posed to stakeholders concerning the question categories mentioned. Stakeholders were asked three basic questions concerning effectiveness factors: (1) To what extent do we engage in this behavior or address this issue? (2) How much will a change in our practices on this item increase the academic achievement of our students? and (3) How much effort will it take to significantly change our practices regarding this issue?

Each of the effectiveness factors are aligned with the three basic questions and rated on a scale indicating "not at all" (1); through "to a great extent" (4). The instrument can be modified and adapted by school districts to meet their unique needs. The content aspects of the questionnaire are the principal component of the proposed model. These components can be modified for African-American males who reside in, as well as attend, urban school districts.

IMPLEMENTING THE MODEL

To be successful, reform models must focus on parents, teachers, students, curriculum development, and stakeholders in the development of goals, solutions, and actions needed to change negative behaviors that may contribute to a significant increase in the number of African-American males being incarcerated. Reform requires collaboration, time, commitment, and deduction between stakeholders.

Assessment of Needs

School districts should conduct systematic assessments with parental input. This will determine factors associated with promoting behavior that may lead to criminal convictions of African-American males. Several types of data-gathering instruments may be used to make sound educational decisions relevant to the issue. The survey instrument developed by Marzano[8] is highly recommended for urban school districts to use in assessing their instructional program. These strategies were addressed earlier in the chapter. In summary, this survey focuses on three questions: (1) How well is the school doing in teaching and motivating learners? (2) How will current or projected practices improve students' achievement? and (3) How much effort will it take to change current practices? Answering these three questions will provide the necessary information for school districts to start effective school reforms in educating African-American males.

The needs assessment should involve instruments to ascertain problems, culture, and norms of the community as viewed by the stakeholders. Another strategy is the use of focus groups to identify problems in the educational program for African-American males. Once the assessed needs of a school district have been determined, they should be prioritized and a team assigned to align the needs with standards.

Formulation of Goals and Objectives

In forming the assessed needs, realistic and functional goals should be developed and aligned with strategies for reducing incarceration. The goals should assist in the selection of objectives, identification of resources needed, and basic skills needed to achieve the objectives. The goals and objectives, in terms of the behaviors and learning styles of African-American males, should be divided into manageable parts so that the males can succeed. Schmoker[9] summed up the discussion by stating that setting academic goals for the school, as a whole, has a powerful coalescing effect on teachers and administrators. "Goals themselves lead not only to success but also to the effectiveness and cohesion of a team."

Little's[10] findings were similar to Schmoker's. Schmoker revealed that shared responsibility for common goals is more important in establishing collegiality than interpersonal friendships; establishing and collaborating on academic goals is essential to effective reforms.

Schmoker listed several considerations that should be employed in establishing school-wide goals. The goals are as follows:

1. Do not develop too many achievement goals; one or two may be enough.

2. Avoid the principle of rapid results; short-term results can be used to develop a foundation to build upon.
3. Establishing goals for individual students is probably more powerful than setting a few school-wide goals.

Curriculum and Instructional Strategies

Goals and objectives should indicate the nature and type of curricula patterns and instructional strategies to be used to instruct the students. Instructional units should be aligned to standards and should take into consideration the needs, capacities, interests, cultural values, and learning styles of African-American males. Teachers of African-American males will need to base curriculum designs and instruction on the unique needs of the students.

Curriculum and instructional strategies should be based upon skills needed for African-American males to function successfully in society. The initial step should be to identify skills that are critical to being successful in society. The second step is to sequence specific objectives as they relate to the general objectives by breaking them down into small, manageable tasks that the boys can achieve. The third step is to identify instructional activities that can achieve the objectives, such as individualized instruction. Computer-assisted instruction, cooperative learning, and direct instruction are but a few. Identification of appropriate resources should complement the instructional strategies. The fourth step is to include cultural, ethnic, and racial diversity into the curriculum, which will enable African-American males to appreciate and understand their self-worth. When individuals feel good about themselves, they generally want to support views held by the general society. Parents should be trained and invited to participate in these steps based upon their background and understanding.

CLOSING THE ACHIEVEMENT GAP

African-American males on the average are behind their peers in achievement due to many factors, as outlined in the introduction. The trend is well noted in kindergarten and rapidly expands during elementary school. Sociological factors also significantly add to the problem of the increasing incarceration rate among African-American males.

Because of outdated textbooks and materials, the achievement gap has increasingly widened. Poor facilities, lack of state-of-the-art technology, inadequate funding, testing bias, lack of motivation on the part of African-American males, inappropriate behaviors, differences in personalities and learning styles, and the lack of community support and involvement are but a few factors responsible for widening the achievement gap between African-American males and their peers.

Several research sources have placed teacher training as a significant factor in widening the achievement gap of African-American males. These sources have indicated that, for the most part, less-than-competent teachers are employed to instruct African-American males academic needs. A sufficient number are not certified and do not meet the standards alluded to in the No Child Left Behind Act.

School districts must be accountable for ensuring that all children, including African-American males, meet standards by closing the achievement gap through offering instructional strategies based upon the students' culture and learning styles. When achievement is raised, inappropriate behaviors will decrease and incarceration rates of African-American males will also decrease. Parents of African-American males, in particular, must protest against the inferiority that still exists in the schools and must demand equality for their children.

STUDENT MOTIVATION

The sociological and psychological environments in which a majority of African-American males reside do not provide much motivation to challenge them to achieve. Over time, individuals are motivated to be success oriented or failure avoidant. The latter appears to operate among African-American males chiefly due to poor environmental conditions. A deprived environment offers few challenges for African-American males to want to be successful.

In general, African-American males have not been given the necessary strategies to promote self-motivation. Parents and educators can promote motivation by: (1) enhancing their boys' self-worth, (2) assessing their boys' achievement levels, (3) providing successful experiences, (4) presenting tasks that are culturally relevant, and (5) explaining, discussing, and modeling the dynamics of motivation and how it can improve their boys' self-worth in society.

Parents must help to make schools in urban communities more tolerant of the cultural and behavioral styles of African-American males, since the learning styles of African-American males are well entrenched by the time they enter school. The factors and traits of the boys must be coordinated and infused into an integrated program to improve self-worth and enhance motivation, as motivation is a prerequisite to learning and developing appropriate social skills to cope successfully in society.

CLASSROOM MANAGEMENT

All children, including African-American males, enter school with wide
ranges of behavioral styles, including interests, motivation, personalities,
learning, cultural styles, and attitudes that play an important role in changing
negative behaviors. These traits and abilities influence positive classroom
behaviors. Parents must be instructed to recognize the differences in the
behavioral styles of their African-American males and plan appropriately.
Frequently, these behavioral styles are inappropriate for the school. The following strategies are recommended for parents, particularly those of African-
American males: (1) provide strategies to raise the boys' tolerance levels by
recognizing causal factors, such as environment, culture, and values and the
impact of these factors on behavior; (2) raise expectation levels for the boys
by expecting them to display positive behaviors (in some instances, positive
behaviors will need to be modeled by both parents and teachers); (3) analyze
their behaviors toward the boys (the boys are skilled at using teachers' overt
behaviors to determine negative and positive reflections); and (4) establish
realistic rules and routines and constantly review them; the roles and routines
should be changed as needed. Make sure the boys fully understand the rules.
Practice should be given where needed.

PARENTAL INVOLVEMENT

The role of parental involvement in reducing the incarceration rate and in
education has proved to be essential. Research findings show that many
parents do not feel welcome in the schools; thus, they believe their participation has little to offer because of lack of education and social graces. Many
parents have transportation problems and work during the school day. Other
reasons cited for the parents' lack of involvement is that they are not familiar
with the instructional program, they do not have appropriate clothes, and
teachers, administrators, and other staff look down on them and treat them
rudely.

Reforms are urgently needed to discover creative ways of involving parents in the education of African-American males; parents must feel welcome
in the schools and invited to be stakeholders. Culture values, education, and
sociological status should have no impact on limiting their involvement.
These and other factors cited must be addressed if parental involvement is to
have a sufficient impact on reducing the incarceration rate.

EARLY CHILDHOOD AND HOME ENVIRONMENT

Lack of early childhood experiences and development issues impede the normal growth and development of African-American males. Some African-American males are, too often, born into poverty and lack sufficient resources, which can seriously impair their abilities to learn. These African-American males' early environmental experiences can interfere with their academic growth and development. Too often, African-American males are born and live in home environments where they are denied appropriate experiences needed for developing positive foundations for learning.

Lack of adequate adult stimulation in the early years can lead to development of negative behaviors, which may be irreversible. African-American males, as well as all children, learn behavior early; unfortunately, many of these behaviors are negative and conflict with standards imposed by the school and society. Parents must become aware of these factors and teach the boys effective ways to deal with negative behaviors, which impact behavior and performance.

FINANCE AND RESOURCES

Most schools that serve African-American males are underfunded. Nationwide, a significant number of schools serving African-American males are Title I schools. Funds may be used to improve instruction in these schools by employing specialists to assist teachers in focusing on goals and objectives that exemplify quality education to African-American males. The lack of finances prohibits schools from providing adequate services and instruction and has been shown to be directly correlated with African-American males' turning to criminal behaviors.

School districts should seek other funds through local and state agencies, both in the public and private sectors, for education personnel, materials, equipment, and training that are needed to equalize educational opportunities for the boys. The strain of tight budgets, in general, makes city school districts suffer disproportionately. Also, eroding tax bases and an over-reliance on local property taxes to finance education virtually guarantees poor and urban areas to lag behind nonurban districts.

Finding the money and resources to address facilities' needs is especially difficult. Also, one of the biggest challenges impacting school facilities and one of the most promising is the development of technology integration. Incorporating technology into schools has proved too difficult for many urban districts due to insufficient funds and inadequate infrastructures.

A recent U.S. Department of Education study on school spending reported that in central cities, where greater numbers of students are in poverty and it costs more to educate them than nonpoor students, schools must spend a greater portion of limited funds on instruction and less on repairing buildings or buying and/or repairing equipment. This has too often led to dangerous infrastructure conditions. Another government study reported that urban school districts spend on average about 3.5 percent of their budgets on facilities maintenance (compared with a national average expenditure of 9.4 percent; 85 percent is spent for emergency repairs). The remaining amount typically is spent on preventive maintenance and dealing with escalating costs to operate and maintain buildings.[11]

NOTES

1. G. R. Taylor, *Curriculum Strategies: Social Skills Intervention for Young African-American Males* (Westport, CT: Greenwood, 1997); G. R. Taylor, *Practical Application of Social Learning Theories in Educating Young African-American Males* (Lanham, MD: University Press of America, 2003); P. E. Dewitt, "The Crucial Early Years," *Time*, April 18, 1994, 68.

2. D. Hopkins and M. Ainscow, "Making Sense of School Improvement: An Interim Account of the IQEA Project." Paper presented at the ESRC seminar series on School Effectiveness and School Improvement. Sheffield Publishers, 1993; Agron (2000).

3. M. Fullan and A. Hargreaves, *What's Worth Fighting for in Your School?* (New York: Teachers College Press, 1996).

4. Reynolds et al. (2000), 223.

5. R. J. Marzano, *Transforming Classroom Grading* (Alexandria, VA: Association for Supervision and Curriculum Development, 2000).

6. R. J. Marzano, *What Works in Schools: Translating Research into Action* (Alexandria, VA: Association for Supervision and Curriculum Development, 2003).

7. Marzano (2003)

8. Marzano (2003)

9. M. Schmoker, *Results: The Key to Continuous School Improvement*, 2nd ed. (Alexandria, VA: Association for Supervision and Curriculum Development, 1999), 24.

10. Taylor (1997, 2003); P. E. Dewitt (1994).

11. Hopkins and Ainscow (1993); Agron (2000).

Chapter Ten

Summary

Self-esteen is a major factor affecting how well we function in our environment. Promoting positive self-esteem among children, and in particular Afircan-American males, assists in reducing problems that might otherwise may surface later in life. Several authorities have advocated for the need of additional research in this area to evaluate the impact of strategies and programs designed to promote positive self-esteem. [1]

Although we still need empirical data on the effectiveness of programs to raise self-esteem among children, high self-esteem appears to promote confidence, security, citizenship, and academic success. Recommended strategies or principles for improving self-esteem include the following:

- Praise rather than criticize.
- Teach children to set achievable goals.
- Teach children to praise themselves and to capitalize on their strong points.
- Teach children to praise others.
- Set realistic expectation levels.
- Teach children to have confidence in themselves.
- Praise children for achieving or failing after attempting to achieve.
- Praise children for successfully completing a test or project.
- Praise children for positive criticism.
- Accept pupils' contributions without judgment.
- Listen to children; they have important information to share.
- Maintain a "you can do it" philosophy.
- Present challenges for children.
- Provide movement and freedom within the classroom for children to achieve objectives.

- Demonstrate and show respect for children.
- Listen to how you talk to children.
- Catch someone doing something right and praise him or her for it.
- Attack the behavior, not the student; separate the behavior from the child.
- Use modeling or other techniques to reduce maladaptive behavior.
- Teach children to respect themselves and others.
- Teach children to be proud of their heritage.
- Provide activities that incorporate involvement.

These strategies are not all inclusive and should be expanded as assessed by the teachers and parents.

Nationwide, African-American males disproportionately live in substandard environments where they are denied appropriate mental, physical, and social stimulations. Parents must work together on a unified front to demand that local and state officials change these substandard conditions which attribute to African-American males' incarceration rates. These conditions also impede normal development in all areas of general functioning. Consequently, direct and immediate intervention must be made in the social environment of these children if they are to profit sufficiently from their school experiences. A significant percentage of schools in urban districts are so dilapidated that they constitute safety hazards for the children attending them. These substandard schools frequently mirror the conditions present in the communities of these boys and deny the boys appropriate mental, physical, and social stimulation.

Facilities in many urban school districts are inferior and plagued with unsafe conditions. They reflect the facilities in the boys' communities and homes. The infrastructure of the schools is generally in a state of decay. Walls, ceilings, and toilets are substandard and are in need of painting and repair. Generally, the schools are not safe. Doors are frequently broken or do not work; the same can be said for the windows. The heating and ventilation systems are usually old and frequently do not work. The conditions of the classrooms and other physical resources in the schools are also below standard when compared with those of suburban schools. The lack of safety regulations will have an adverse effect upon learning and the social and physical environment of the home and school. Both the home and school have failed to provide safe environments in most urban school districts. African-American males need a safe environment that shelters them, promotes learning, and assists in closing the achievement gap.[2]

As mentioned earlier in the book, the gap in education is the greatest in poor neighborhoods. Children from deprived homes and neighborhoods do not leave the miseries at home when they go to school. Schools too often reflect the poverty the children experience in their neighborhoods. They mostly enter schools less ready to learn due to these ecological and social factors, and may begin to lag behind at an early age. Unfortunately, due to unequal playing fields, many African-American males face higher rates of health, physical, social, and psychological problems. These problems significantly contribute to poverty, dropping out of school, drug use, crime, and early pregnancies[3] as well as decreasing the children's well-being and safety in the schools.

As indicated, the aforementioned problems do not apply to all African-American males. Many overcome the barriers in their social, personal, and academic lives to succeed in school and later in their careers. A significant percentage of them are not at risk. They live in environments that promote self-esteem and self-activity with appropriate models to emulate.

Due to the various factors within the society and the community, the parent's role in enhancing self-esteem is of prime importance. Intervention must be made early to break or prevent failure due to low self-esteem. Thus, there appears to be a positive relationship between self-concept and a student's success or failure in school.[4]

Many factors influence African-American males' development prior to going to school. When the school accepts the child, it should be committed to accepting and attempting to teach the whole child, not just developing the three *R*'s. A major factor in children's development in the beginning school years is the view they have of themselves as they communicate with other students. For African-American males as well as other students, self-concept influences the motivation to learn. If students do not feel good about themselves generally and good about themselves specifically as learners, then they will lack the motivation to improve their performance in many academic areas. Group and individual activities are needed in order to improve the self-concepts of African-American males.

The role of the parents in promoting self-control cannot be overemphasized. They must insist that the school infuse social and self-control skills in instruction. Specifically, the parent exerts considerable influence on a child's self-concept through the types of treatment, beliefs, and expectations the parent puts on the child. Children quickly react to and interpret negative traits projected by the parent. The child's interpretation of the parent's actions and their significance plays an important role in how the child reacts and participates in keeping the environment safe.

Children sift, seek, reject, and avoid information from individuals they do not respect or trust. Thus, they do not accept information from adults who have rejected them as readily as they do from adults whom they feel have accepted them and seem trustworthy. Parents can exert significant influence on the forming of the child's self-concept by constructing and nurturing a positive and safe learning environment, as well as showing positive attitudes and developing rapport with children.

The socioeconomic status of children should have no effect on how their ability to learn is judged. One major condition for enhancing self-esteem in the child is the parent's acceptance of the child. By accepting the child, the parent indicates to the child that he or she is worthy of the parent's attention and respect.[5]

The home environment provides the necessary support, safety, and love for appropriate social and emotional development to occur.[6] Intervention and strategies outlined and discussed in this text are designed to improve interpersonal and academic skills of African-American males who are at risk. Presidents Obama, Clinton, and Ford were instrumental in passing laws to improve educational opportunities for African-American males. Creating a safe environment for learning to occur and increasing funding were two of the major issues outlined.

DRUGS

There is a significant relationship between drug addiction and criminal behavior, which frequently leads to the incarceration of African-American males. Parents should receive instructions from the school and community agencies on techniques for preventing drug use by the males. Drug use by African-American males is rampant and responsible for many violent, aggressive, and inappropriate acts.[7] Drugs are responsible for many violent, aggressive, and inappropriate acts, which frequently create unsafe environments. Short[8] concluded that there is a relationship between violent crime, drug crime, lower socioeconomic status, and black males and offers an explanation of this relationship.

First, Short[9] reports that the distribution of violent crimes associated with drugs is heavily skewed toward younger, poorer, male minorities. Community variables, such as the availability of job opportunities and the dominant beliefs and values transmitted in a neighborhood, strongly interact with microsocial variables to produce violent behavior. The school and social agencies should provide training to parents that is relevant to recommended strategies that they can use to combat drug use, which is responsible for unsafe acts performed by the boys.

Short[10] further claimed that prominent among the effects of these community variables is the presence of unsupervised youth groups or gangs. Short argues that gangs emerge in situations in which traditional kinds of social capital have eroded because of demographic and economic shifts that concentrate poverty and destabilize conventional community institutions. In such situations, Short states that

The legitimacy of adults associated with these institutions is weakened, and young people become more likely to resist adult authority. This situation breeds the conditions for violent behavior at the microlevel. Included in salient microlevel variables are the presence of early childhood disorders, alcoholism and drugs, marital discord, and impulsive and aggressive behavior.

A related explanation for the involvement of lower-class African-American males in drug crime has been offered by Manwar,[11] who articulated that cross-cultural studies have found that children deprived of parental affection tend to become aggressive, and during the formative phase, these circumstances shape and mold personality. Manwar further notes that in U.S. inner cities, especially in the African-American community, the process of identity formation is different from that in the mainstream culture. The point is that since poverty, social discrimination, violence, crime, and drug use are prevalent in the inner cities, they play a vital role in the process of identity formation. Violent acts caused by drug use frequently create unsafe conditions in the learning environment.

In particular, two kinds of structural conditions, economic and ideological, are said to determine the youth's involvement with violence, crime, and drug selling and/or use. In this cultural environment, aggressive behavior (e.g., counterhegemonic confrontation with the elite culture and equivocation of state control) is viewed as a powerful attribute for a person. Manwar[12] stated that it is this kind of identity that leads to the involvement of young, poor African-American males in drug crime.

Palermo and Simpson's[13] argument finds some support in a study of drugs and crime in a sample of upper-middle-class adolescents (both African-American and white) conducted by Levine and Kozak.[14] Findings of the study indicated that the drug-related crimes committed by these young people ruled out the explanations usually offered to explain lower socioeconomic involvement in drug crime (e.g., unemployment, negative social conditions, and so forth). It is essential that parents be knowledgeable about drug use and intervention strategies based on findings from this study. Parents should also be apprised of the psychological factors associated with drug abuse.

PSYCHOLOGICAL FACTORS ASSOCIATED WITH DRUG ABUSE

There are several psychological factors associated with drug abuse habits. These factors significantly impact treatments, which impact social development. Drugs have been found to have a severe impact upon the psychological development of African-American males as well as other individuals. Psychological factors affect a wide range of relationships, including (1) par-

ent-child interactions, (2) peer relationships that influence drug-related behaviors and place African-American males at risk for experimenting with
drugs, and (3) relationships with adult role models who, as in peer relations,
influence how children react to drugs. Youths frequently model the behaviors
of adults they admire. Special social intervention strategies may be used to
reduce, minimize, or eradicate the use of drugs, which is rampant among
African-American males.

One key to breaking the vicious drug cycle is the education of African-
American males directed toward the prevention of drug use and the rehabili-
tation of drug users, with emphasis on the causes and consequences of drug
misuse and abuse. An attempt to reduce drug use and to create a safe environment was made in goal 6 of the National Goals for Education,[15] which
focused on every school in America being free of drugs and violence and
offering a safe, disciplined environment conducive to learning by 2000. Although bold attempts were made, this goal has not been achieved. Additionally, federal legislation and grants have been made to school districts to assist
them in achieving the goal. Both parents and the school must collaborate to
reach this end.

INCREASED BUDGET ALLOCATIONS

Parents must become politically active to demand that additional funds be
allocated to repair dilapidated buildings to make them safe. State-of-the-art
technology must be purchased. The present method of financing urban
school districts places them at a great disadvantage for appropriately educating African-American males. Due to the needs of this population and smaller
resources to draw from, the school does not receive equal funding compared
with funding for suburban schools.

To ensure that urban school districts that serve African-American males
receive equal funding, parents must demand changes in local and state funding patterns. One recommended procedure would be for the state to provide
tuition vouchers to parents, similar to those outlined in the No Child Left
Behind Act, PL. 107-110. Parents would be free to use the vouchers at any
school in the school district. Additional funding and vouchers will be of little
use unless competent teachers, resources, safe environments, and prerequisite skills are in place in order to achieve the stated standards.

SUMMARY

Many African-American males attend unsafe schools due to many factors. Parents have little control over unsafe schools. These factors significantly impede learning and promote all forms of deviant behaviors. Parents must become politically active and demand that schools serving African-American males be made as safe as other schools in affluent communities. A safe, supportive environment tends to facilitate learning. Prosocial skills taught and practiced daily in a nurturing environment assist in reducing negative behaviors and in promoting positive ones.[16]

All children, as well as African-American males, need a safe environment to help them learn and to shelter them. One of the most challenging issues plaguing urban school districts is a deteriorating and aging educational infrastructure. Drugs, violence, and outdated equipment also may constitute safety problems. These problems can significantly impede learning. Children must feel safe in the school environment. The federal government has attempted to enforce safety in the schools through goal 6. Goal 6 stated that by the year 2000, every school in America would be free of drugs and violence and would offer a disciplined environment conducive to learning. Unfortunately, this goal has not been achieved in many urban school districts.

Public schools cannot achieve this goal alone. Widespread local, state, and federal support is needed. Collaboration between the school systems, parents, communities, and stakeholders is needed to form teams to develop strategies to make the schools safe for children and educational personnel through workshops and meetings. These gatherings should apprise parents of the issues and facts concerning unsafe schools, deteriorating infrastructure, allocating resources, locations in deprived communities, poor environmental conditions, drugs, violence, crime, outdated equipment, and increased budget allocations. If implemented, these strategies will have a significant impact on decreasing the incarceration rates of African-American males.

NOTES

1. G. R. Taylor, "Impact of Social Learning Theory on Educating Deprived/Minority Children," Clearinghouse for Teacher Education (Washington, DC: ERIC ED 349260, 1992).

2. G. R. Taylor, *Classroom Management Theories into Practice* (Lanham, MD: University Press of America, 2004).

3. K. Vail, "Grasping What Kids Need to Raise Performance," *American School Board Journal* 190 (2003): 46–52; J. D. Finn, *School Engagement and Students at Risk* (National Center for Educational Statistics, 2002).

4. G. R. Taylor, *Black Male Project* (report submitted to Sinclair Lane Elementary School, Baltimore, MD, 1993).

5. G. R. Taylor, *Practical Application of Social Learning Theories in Educating Young African-American Males* (Lanham, MD: University Press of America, 2003).

6. W. C Ayers, *The Good Preschool Teacher: Six Teachers Reflect on Their Lives* (New York: Teachers College Press, 1989); S. Kagan, "The Structural Approach to Cooperative Learning," *Educational Leadership* 47(14) (1990): 12–15.

7. M. Mauer and T. Huling, *Young Black Americans and the Criminal Justice System: Five Years Later* (Washington, DC: The Sentencing Project, 1995), 19. http://www.sentencing project.org/policy/19070.html; P. Greenwood, "Substance Abuse among High-Risk Youth and Potential Intervention," *Crime and Delinquency* 38(4) (1992): 444–58; U.S. Department of Justice, Bureau of Justice Statistics, *Sentencing in the Federal Courts: Does Race Matter? The Transition to Sentencing Guidelines, 1986–1990* (Washington, DC: U.S. Government Printing Office, 1993); Taylor (1993); J. F. Short, *Poverty, Ethnicity, and Violent Crime* (Boulder, CO: Westview Press, 1997).

8. Short (1997).

9. Short (1997).

10. Taylor (1992).

11. Taylor (1992).

12. Taylor (1992).

13. Taylor (1992).

14. Taylor (1992).

15. Taylor (1992).

16. Taylor (1992).

Index

About the Authors

Dr. Theresa L. Harris is an associate professor at Coppin State University in Baltimore, Maryland. She has served as the chairperson of the Adult and General Education Department. Dr. Harris has more than two decades of varied experience in education, counseling, and criminal justice. She has assisted State of Maryland departments, including the departments of education and criminal justice, local education, and private sector organizations, and worked with individual schools in formulating strategies and practices for implementing successful changes in the academic outcomes of student performance. With an earned doctorate degree in social psychology/sociology from Howard University as well as continuing education credits provided by the Johns Hopkins School of Medicine and the Board of Professional Counsleors in social work, Dr. Harris has used her education and training to support grassroots-level community projects, sponsored research, and acted as a consultant to governmental agencies. She has studied abroad on a number of occasions and has used this experience to support global international educational dialogue and experiences for her students.

Dr. George R. Taylor is professor of special education, chairperson of the Department of Special Education, and acting dean for the School of Education at Coppin State University. His knowledge and expertise in the areas of special education, research, and educational psychology are both locally and nationally renowned. Dr. Taylor has made significant contributions to these fields by publishing more than twenty professional articles and twenty-one textbooks.

CPSIA information can be obtained at www.ICGtesting.com
Printed in the USA
BVOW012247210212

283485BV00002B/1/P

9 781607 092988